Organize

How to Declutter Your Home and Keep It That Way

(How to Manage Your Day and to Become More Productive and Successful)

Daniel McGrath

Published By **Oliver Leish**

Daniel McGrath

All Rights Reserved

Organize: How to Declutter Your Home and Keep It That Way (How to Manage Your Day and to Become More Productive and Successful)

ISBN 978-1-998769-27-8

Legal & Disclaimer

Table of contents

Chapter 1: Before You Begin _____ 1

Chapter 2: Configure Your Digital Filing System _____ 23

Chapter 3: Financial Relevancies _____ 82

Chapter 4: Keeping The Paper-Free Office For The Foreseeable Future _____ 92

Chapter 5: Organizing Your Mind_____ 99

Chapter 6: What Is The Best Way Do We Begin To Organization In Our Lives? __ 122

Chapter 7: Importance Organizing Your Life _____ 153

Chapter 1: Before you begin

Do not declare bankruptcy on paper.

It's tempting to declaring "paper bankruptcy" and throw your papers out, without having a second look. While I'm sure that the world wouldn't cease to exist if you did that however, I wouldn't suggest the idea.

It's true that you do not require the bulk of your papers.

Also, if you accidentally throw away something you actually require, the majority of times you can change the file.

Now you're thinking that the paper bankruptcy market is getting better and better.

Remember that the replacement of a document can cost both the time as well as money. If you happen to shred the birth certificate, you're able to get another. However, you'll need pay a fee and depending on the state the birth certificate was issued in, it could be a trouble. The same applies to vehicle titles. You can get a replacement for the title of your vehicle however, it's a hassle and will incur an expense.

You might also have papers that's valuable. If you've inherited papers from your family member or spouse or friend, you may have banks or financial instruments which you're not aware of. If you decide to throw the file away without examining it then you'll not be able to tell the difference however it's not a risk you'd like to take.

Last but not least, I mentioned that the majority of the paper documents you have are re-usable. However, not all documents are similar to the other. There might be correspondence you'd like to look over to preserve your memories. You may have legal documents that were created without the help of an attorney and consequently, not shared with one. It is possible to find legal documents that were created by an attorney, however in the event that you've lost the name of the attorney then you'll not be able to figure out who to contact to retrieve it. There might be key codes or passwords which cannot be duplicated. For instance, items such as home security software or computer safes usually have key codes that were made available on paper. If you do not have the key code and you don't have the key code, you cannot reinstall the software or buy an additional key for your safe.

So, even if you are faced with an overwhelming amount of paper to separate however, I would still suggest that you do not dump it all out.

Know your personal timeline and know your goals.

You'll need to move forward in digitizing your document in accordance with your personality and the quantity of paper you own and the kind of paper you've got and the amount of time you'll need to spend.

Certain people are more comfortable doing a job for a short period of time. It could be as little as thirty minutes per week, or 10-15 minutes per week until they're done. Choose what works for you. If you're a huge pile of papers, it's acceptable to work slowly when you have time. It could take a few months, but that's acceptable!

Some people are prone to working on a small amount at an time, and want to finish the task in the shortest time possible...or might need to digitally digitize their paper fast to meet the deadline for moving out.

Do you have relatives or friends who could assist you? If you have people who you trust, particularly people who are great at managing things. They will keep you on track or organize your papers for you. This is a great option when you want to digitize your papers and/or photographs quickly.

Consider your budget

There are a variety of tools available to assist you in setting up your paper-free filing system. Some are completely free, while others cost money. Based on your individual situation along with the volume of paper you own to work with, consider how much money you're willing to invest in establishing your system. It does not need to be a huge amount of money However, using some paid-for tools can help speed up the process.

For the majority of projects at a minimum, you'll require the scanner (or smartphone) and a computer and a binder to store your remaining papers. Additionally, you should use a password manager and the offsite (or cloud) storage account, as well as shredder for paper. You might be able to borrow the tools through your workplace, colleague or even from the library in your area. I'll discuss all options available to use these tools within the following chapter.

You'll need tools
Smartphones or scanners

You'll need a method to digitalize your paper and there are more aspects to take into consideration than you think. What amount of paper are you digitizing? Do you have a mix of photos and paper? What's your preferred format of the image (PDF, JPG, or both)? Are your papers printed double-sided?

It is possible to get an ultra-fast scanner to scan the paper you're using currently, and then switch to your smartphone in the future. You may also decide that you need to purchase a scanner. There are a variety of options to choose from.

* If you're working with small paper and are using a smartphone, there are a number of alternatives for making digital photos from your papers. Modern phones with the most current software have scanning capabilities built-in. Phones can be scanned as PDF files and also send the send the scan to Dropbox meaning you don't have to go through the additional steps to remove the image from your phone. Android phones can upload

photos of files to Google Drive. You can also make JPG pictures of the document by simply taking pictures of each document.

Pros: Free

Cons: slow and you must remove the images from your smartphone if they are not being uploaded direct into Dropbox and Google Drive, image quality is dependent on your personal photographic skills.

There are numerous scanner programs that are available, which is especially helpful for earlier model smartphone that doesn't run the most recent software. Certain apps offer an initial trial period for free. It is still necessary to take photographs of each document, but with this app, you are able to convert the PDF to a PDF, or join multiple pages and utilize OCR (optical character recognition) which allows you to look up your documents.

Pros: trial for free PDF option is helpful OCR option can be useful

Pros: could be costly after a no-cost trial ($10 monthly subscription) It can also be filled with ads, time-consuming image quality may not be the greatest

* Document scanners that are handheld "wands" are made of a ruler however, they are only approximately an inch high. They feature a glass window at the bottom, and you are able to physically push the scanner over your photo or paper. Think of a photocopier, only you're in charge of shifting the scanner with your arm. This can be a challenge to create a quality image, so some experience is required. The cost is between $50 and $100. They are intended to be portable and don't require to be connected to laptops.

Pros: Low cost, compact and portable. Computer isn't required for scanning in the event that it can save the image onto the SD memory card.

Pros: hard to use, lengthy images are not the best. You still need to transfer your images off your SD card.

* Small portable document scanners are similar to wads, however each sheet of paper goes to the scanner instead of having to move the device over on top. These scanners cost between $100 to $150 and

deliver excellent results. I suggest you look for the Brother brand portable document scanner. I have an older version , and frequently use it and I highly recommend it. The latest model comes with more features that can make scanning effortless, and continue to be useful for the papers you receive. The Brother scanner brand includes software that you can use to manage all your files on digital, but you do not have to install it.

Pros: Simple to use, high-quality images, extremely compact size, multiple output options, quick scanning. Newer models come with dual-sided scanning which means it's not necessary turn the pages to view both sides of the page. Color or black and white scanning. Some scanners have SD cards that are included, so you don't need to plug into laptops.

Pros: more expensive cost, only handle photos or pages that can be fed into this machine (no books or documents that are fragile) and no document feeder.

Flatbed scanners consume lots of desk space They are great for scanning multiple images, books simultaneously, or delicate documents that you don't need to pass through the document feeder. If you're looking at flatbed scanners, make sure finding one that comes with the option of an automated document feeder (ADF) in addition to the flatbed scanning feature. Otherwise, it's very slow because you'll need to manually insert one document at a time to the scanner. Flatbed scanners cost between $70 and $250 and beyond. They're not always the best choice unless you already own one, or you are able to find a used scanner at an affordable cost. All-in-one printer/copier/scanners have more functionality and tend to be cheaper.

Pros: Excellent to scan items that cannot be handled by the scanner on a mobile device, for instance books and fragile documents. It is easy to use. Could have a document scanner for quick scanning of the paper stacks.

Pros slow scanning when there's no ADF or scanner. Also, the price is higher and occupies a lot of desk space.

* All-in-one printer/copier/scanners are basically printers that serve a few other functions. Find one that has an ADF which is particularly beneficial when the ADF can work with double-sided papers (i.e. that the ADF can flip the document to scan the two sides of the page in right sequence). This all-in-one scanner can function as a flatbed scanner as well as a normal paper scanner. They cost around $130.

Pros: Multi-function, If you plan to purchase one, with a reasonable price for its functionality, high-quality scans.

Pros: The biggest size of all the options, which is too much for an scanner.

The best practice is to use an ultra-compact portable document scanner if intend to spend dollars. They're small and provide high-quality scans, and last for a long duration because they contain the least number of parts that break. I've had one of the Brother brand for several years and it has not broken. One time I had to replace an USB cord that connected it to my computer.

When we began the medical practice, we also put in a massive all-in-one scanner/printer. I use it often as it has an ADF. But I was disappointed that we erroneously selected a scanner which does not scan each side of the document when you use the ADF. This means that I need to scan the paper stack before turning over the paper and scan again. The result is an assortment of pages that aren't in order. Since I don't often have to use my filing paper it's not an issue. However, it it can be a minor inconvenience. I'd rather this rather than scan each side in a separate way.

If you don't have more than $100 to purchase scanners, consider the possibility of borrowing one from a family member or a neighbor (try the community message board) or your employer or even the library. A lot of libraries have the "library of items" which could include a scanner for documents. When you've got the bulk of your scanning completed, you can continue to use your paper-free system by using your smartphone.

A computer

You can use a desktop computer or a laptop computer. But you'll require a space you control and own in which all the documents you scan will be stored.

Some examples of things that you do not have control over include: the laptop belonging to the company you work for, laptop belonging to your partner or your friend cloud storage that includes email servers. I've witnessed individuals constantly losing their files due to the fact that they considered these types that they stored as personal possessions.

A method for backing up your files

Your hard drive or computer will surely end up failing or becoming obsolete at some point. A paper-free system implies that you have to back up your data. As "two is one and one is not enough" is the saying. Here are some methods to backup your scanned documents.

Buy an external flash drive or hard drive, and copy/paste your scan documents to it regularly. Make a reminder in your calendar to remind you to copy/paste. Of obviously, the external hard drive could be vulnerable to failure. However, it's unlikely that it will fail exactly at the identical time that your PC does. External drives are also vulnerable to fire, theft, etc.

Pros: Relatively affordable price for storage device, either a flash or hard disk. It's easy to drag and drop your scanned files onto.

Cons: Also susceptible to failure. If you store your backups close to your computer, it is susceptible to loss. Backups aren't always automatic.

Copy/paste the scanned files into a cloud-based application or server, like Dropbox, Evernote, icloud as well as Google Drive. Send scanned images to yourself. Scanned images are able to be uploaded on a photo hosting service like Shutterfly.

Pros: Free simple to use, when you don't have many files

The files are beyond your control. If the hosting company shuts down or suffers from a data breach you may lose your backup data. Backups aren't automatically.

Subscription to an automatic backup service, like Carbonite as well as Microsoft OneDrive.
Pros: Automatic, "set it and forget it" backups. The ability to access all your data online.
Pros: Not free. As with all offsite storage, you cannot prevent loss caused by hackers, data breaches or other actions by Hosting companies.
Best Practice: A combination of all the above. I back up my laptop onto an external drive every month. I schedule a calendar reminder to make it happen on the 1st of every month. Then, I plug in the drive using the USB cable and then drag/drop my laptop drive across. It takes around an hour due to the sheer amount of files I own. I prefer the method using hard drives since it's entirely under my control.

Each month I upload my pictures to Shutterfly. I've been using Shutterfly for years and am confident in that they won't shut down without warning. We'll discuss more pictures in a future chapter.

In the end, I'm paying for a subscription to Carbonite. I've used Carbonite for several years and have confidence in the service. The files are saved in real-time, and I am able to access them via the internet even when I'm not at my desk. If my computer breaks it is possible to restore all my files from Carbonite.

I only upload a small amount in files through Dropbox along with Evernote. I utilize Dropbox for only files I may need to quickly review on my mobile. I seldom use it for other purposes. I love Evernote because it can apply OCR to everything and therefore it's ideal for documents that I tear out of magazines. It allows me to search for keywords and quickly discover the article in the future. I will provide more details on these apps in the future.

If you can't afford to sign up for an automatic cloud backup service you should at a minimum, back up your documents to an external drive and make sure to store the drive in a different location. If you lose your computer during a fire, for instance it would be backed up to a backup drive that will remain accessible.

A password manager

The paper-free office is that you'll accessing certain documents on the internet via an app or website that is password-secured. Additionally, you will require an account that you can save the account numbers and other information without needing to reference the paper.

The password manager can be described as a program or application that can store your passwords in one place, so that you don't need to keep them in a notebook or record the passwords.

For a long time I was reluctant to use an account manager for passwords. I was sure it wasn't secure using the exact same password for all of my accounts and so I attempted to come up with an algorithm that I only knew. It didn't end up working either since some applications have a 10 character password. certain required 15, while others required specific characters...and my algorithm failed me.

I have reviewed several password management programs and the one I have been using and love for many years is KeePass. The reason I prefer KeePass more than other password managers is that it's not in the cloud, so I have complete control over the location of my data. KeePass is an application that can be downloaded to your computer. It requires a password in order to access KeePass which is the only password you have to remember. KeePass is completely free and can be downloaded from keepass.info.

The only drawback of KeePass I've discovered is that, since I keep the password on my computer, when I want to type an account password on my phone or other device, I must visit my laptop to find the password. This isn't a major issue for me since it doesn't come frequently. It's a matter of keep in mind.

You might be wondering what KeePass differs from entering your passwords into the password-protected Word or Excel document. The main differentiator is KeePass was created specifically for security of passwords, whereas Microsoft Office (and related) products weren't. Therefore, it's a question of picking the best tool to do the task.

Binder(s) to store your remaining papers

As I said before there will be some leftover paper. Most likely, you'll have some form of identification such as birth certificate, passport and social security card. Your title to your vehicle if own your vehicle. Based on your age and your stage of life this could be the case or you might possess additional documents like medical directives and various other documents that are legal. It's still great to keep physical albums of your photos isn't it?

When I first began digitizing my papers I had just one binder with three rings, and it was filled with recipes. It was that simple. This is because my bank provides me a safety deposit box, and I store important documents and car title there.

Recently, I purchased an extra 3-ring binder. It holds paper copies of identification documents, important records, insurance documents medical directives, wills and so on. The binder is redundant since all of these documents are digital or stored in my safe storage box in the banking institution. It came to my mind that in the event of an emergencies, or in the event that I was ill or incapable to speak on my own, the paper binder could be helpful. It's easy to access when I'm forced to leave in a hurry, and also for me or caregiver to access without needing to be able use my digital documents.

In the end, I have photo albums as well as a binder with artwork from the time my kids were small. The albums are all stored digitally, which means that even if they went missing due to fire, they're truly lost. It's nice to go through the physical albums and I'm keeping the books. We'll go over pictures in more depth in a subsequent chapter.

Paper shredders or places to store paper for shredding later

If you're not able to handle a lot of paper it is likely that you'll require shredder. The price starts at with a price of around $40. If you own an office in a medical setting as I do it is recommended to buy the highest quality shredder. It is priced approximately $100.

If you aren't keen to buy a shredder you can place your sensitive papers in boxes and then take it to an UPS retailer or office equipment stores for shredding. They charge around $25 per filing box.

You could also burn paper if there is an appropriate method to do this, or even tear it into pieces and mix it with used dog or cat waste.

The community you live in may also host an event that is free to shred every now and then. If you'd like to take part in thisevent, bear in mind that you'll be required to keep your papers in a place until you're ready for the event to start, and you might have to stand in a line for a while when the day arrives.

The best practice is to buy a shredder that costs $40.
An ideal place to keep your legally binding papers

Paper will continue to enter your home. You can quickly scan and then shred. Certain documents require urgent action. It could be papers such as the school permit slips you give your children and bills that have to be paid via mail or other forms that need your signature. Find out where you're planning to store the papers that need to be kept temporarily. There is a small amount of this kind of paper, therefore it could be in a basket on your desk , or the kitchen table.

Chapter 2: Configure Your digital filing system

Make sure you be aware of your scanner

You are already familiar with the equipment you'll employ to create your paperless system. In addition, you have already purchased the scanner.

It is the next stage to get comfortable using your scanner and then to begin setting your digital folders. Of course, you are able to create folders or alter your directory at any point. However, you should practice on some paper at first to see where your scanner places the file that it scans, as well as what the name of the file is. This information can assist you in making decisions about where to place your directory.

My portable Brother scanner stores documents in a folder was created when on the very first day I used it. The folder is titled "My Scans". It seemed like a good idea to me and I decided to create every sub-folder within my "My Scans" folder of my directory. This means that when I am using my mobile Brother scanner, I'll have less work to complete, namely moving my files into a sensible subfolder.

My all-in-one printer/copier/scanner puts scans into the "Photos" folder in my Windows directory. It's not the place I typically save my documents that I have scanned and it's an additional step to get them from this folder. Photos folder.

If you don't like the default destination your scanner is using, then see whether you can alter the destination.

For Windows users If you have several computers at home or in a very small business and you wish to share your digital cabinet across your network, I suggest creating your digital file directory to be in the Public folder. You can locate it in the Users folder on the C drive of your computer.

If you're scanning with your phone which scans direct into an Dropbox directory or another cloud-based service, ensure you are aware of the steps to alter the directory when needed. Because I don't suggest relying in cloud-based storage services, be sure you understand how to download duplicate files from Dropbox onto your personal computer.

If you're scanning with your phone, but it is also transferring images from the smartphone to your PC, ensure you are aware of how to do this and where to move the files.

In all instances, make sure to ensure the image quality is checked and file size. It is common to choose between either black-and-white or color. It is also possible to alter the dpi settings to cut down on the size of your file. Memory for computers is cheap nowadays, so you do not need to reduce size to save money. However, some scanners be slower to scan when you choose the higher dpi number. Test to find the quality of your image as well as scan speed and the file size you are comfortable with.

If your scanner supports both PDF as well as JPG formats, you should know ways to convert between them.

Also, consider the best way to deal with documents with several pages. I've once contracted a scanning task to a third party and was disappointed with the outcomes. Each report that was scanned contained 4 pages. The outcomes I received were four distinct JPGs per report. This would've made it easier for me to study the reports had they been provided to me as an PDF file with four pages. Many scanners have the option of scanning stacks of paper either as a single PDF or in separate pdfs per page. (Typically you can choose the JPG option will require each page to be a separate document.) Learn about how your scanner operates to ensure that your files are processed effectively and precisely how you'd like them.
Create your file directory

Once you know the scanner's workings You can now create a new directories of files on your personal computer. Utilize your previous documents as a reference point.

Your file directory could be similar to the existing cabinet for files, or you could use it in order to design your own system. If you've never put the file directory then you should take a look at this sample to get ideas. It is best to have a base idea of your directory since you can expand it, or modify it at any time while you scan your paper.

Concerning the names of files...

The scanner assigns file names that don't have any significance for example, BRW0001, BRW0002, etc.

You may be tempted to change the file's name to make it more relevant. In most situations, it is not needed. Incorporate some meaning to your folders for files and you will not need to give any significance to the names of your files.

There may also be software installed on your computer that lets you view pictures of PDFs or JPGs without opening them. This reduces the necessity to change file names to make them easier to find.

Let me provide you with an illustration. Even in the modern age there is a significant amount of paper that is created for medical visits even though electronic documents are available. When I setup my Medical Documentation folder, I'll set up subfolders to each members of the family, just as you can see in the sample directory of files. I could create the file directory exactly as it is and then drop the files into each family members' file folders as they move to my house. There is a good chance that I will never revisit the paper and it's unnecessary to change the name of each file. I can instruct my computer to organize my files by date of scan which means they'll be sorted chronologically in any case. If I want to locate the exact date when my daughter's had her 3rd birthday examination, I won't need to open a lot of documents to find the right one.

When I've got a relative who is prone to frequent medical appointments, I may create subfolders for certain dates or years. Each folder will just contain a few JPGs or PDFs. As an example:

In this instance suppose that in 2019 , I suffered from an issue that led to numerous doctor visits, lab tests, and surgery. The result was much more paper than my annual physicals in 2018 and in 2020. As I scan my papers for these events, I'll create an additional folder for them. I after that, I drag and drop the scans in the appropriate folder.

Even the case that I was able to have lab tests completed four times in the year 2019 I won't need to rename the folders "lab test Jan", "lab test June" and so on. In the "lab test results" folder will contain only four files and I'm probably not going to go back to them. If I did need to look up those January results from the lab I'd be able to locate it quickly, either by studying the dates on the scans of the four documents and even needed to go through each of the four documents.

As you begin to scan, you will be able to determine what is most effective for you. Remember that nobody suggested you should change the name of your files!

The seven categories of paper as well as the three types of paper filers
In this chapter , I'll look at different types of papers you'll come across. There is no need to categorize your paper before you go through it, though you might consider it helpful. It's just important to be aware of the various kinds of papers to ensure that you're better equipped to handle the papers whenever you come across them.

7 Categories of Paper 7 Categories of Paper

The majority of papers can be classified into the seven categories. The idea of categorizing them can help you establish rules for the way you will handle the work as you see it.

1. Vital documents (birth certificates and marriage certificates) Forms of identification (social security cards passports, social security cards) Legal documents (divorce documents medical advance directives, wills and incorporation of a business).
2. Medical records like bills, insurance documents and treatment plans laboratory results, records from office visit, vaccination records.
3. Financial records include bank statements as well as credit card statements utility bills, check statements, tax returns for income and all the supporting documents.

4. Paper that is related to the things that you own, like the pets you have, as well as your home and everything inside. The paper contains receipts and warranties, user guides and maintenance records and also purchases that are that are related to your home.
5. Paper that you intend to refer to later on - recipes or articles that have been cut from

magazines. Rebates and coupons. Notes and lists of tasks to yourself. Lunch menus and school schedules. Magazines you've not read, as well as magazines you've read.

6. Memory – greeting cards, letters, ticket stubsand tickets, school flyers for events in the past Old church directories, artwork that your kids created. Photo albums and photos.

7. Papers that are actionable - issues that require to be dealt with quickly for example, school permit slips, forms that need to be completed.

Once you're familiar with the seven types of paper, your work will be much simpler since you'll have guidelines for yourself to handle each kind. We'll do this in the following section, however first, we have to identify the type of paper filer you are.

The three kinds of paper filers.

There are three kinds of individuals who're looking to set up an office that is paper-free.

There is a generation of young adults who do not have much paper at the moment and would like to start their journey by using a paper-free system. It could be someone who is a Generation Z member, a student, or even a young couple moving into their first home.

Then, there are families or small companies that have many papers and most of the paper is owned by members of the household. That is, you were not the one who inherited this document. This paper was accumulated by you during your lifetime, or the business of yours.

In addition, there are people who inherit paper from a decedent or in the caregiver's role. It is necessary to handle papers, but you're not knowledgeable about the paper as you did not create it.

It is possible to be in more over one categories in the event that you've inherited documents from someone else. I have different ways of dealing with your own documents vs. documents that you have inherited and I have divided them into two separate chapters.

Guidelines for each type of paper
This chapter is specifically geared towards those who are new to the world with little paper as well as households who have produced a large amount of paper for themselves , their immediate family members, or for their small-scale businesses. Paper can fill many filing cabinets or boxes, and could be decades or years old.

If you have inherited papers from a loved one this chapter will give you a baseline guideline for the document. The next chapter provides additional guidelines specific to papers that were inherited.
Purge if you can. Make a plan to deal with anxiety.

Before we discuss the seven different types of paper, and the best way to handle every type of paper I'm giving you the right to eliminate the paper, without scanning it while you work through this procedure.

"Wait," you are thinking. "I'm terrified to eliminate all papers. She assured me that I wasn't required to decide anything on this!" And this is the case. You can begin scanning today. Grab a piece of paper scan it, move the digital file into the appropriate folder and then shred or recycle the paper document and repeat.

As you are doing this, you might begin to feel relaxed and realize that certain papers don't need to be stored in any way. It can save you energy and time to simply take the paper to the recycling bin or shredder without scanning it.

If at any point you are worried about making a choice about whether or not to go through the process, then the general rule should be to go through the process. It will only cost you just a few minutes of your time therefore there is no reason to be anxious about any choice.

However it's possible to find that anxiety isn't triggered through indecision, but rather by certain types of papers. It is possible that you have some negative memories of the event that led to the paper. It's normal. Allow yourself to be tolerant. Do not look at the papers when they cause pain to you. Keep them in a container or in a separate pile. have someone else take them to scan for you or scan them as quickly as you can without looking at the content, and then bring the entire pile in the trash.

It is also possible to find documents that cause guilt for the amount of money you spent or projects that haven't been completed. We've been there. Let yourself be forgiven.

Let's look at the seven different types of paper as well as the best method of dealing with each.

CATEGORY 1: VITAL RECORDS AND LEGAL DOCUMENTS

When you're going through your documents, keep an in mind important documents like birth certificates and adoption documents wedding documents, divorce decrees or death certificates. You'll definitely need to scan copies of thesedocuments, however, you should keep the originals as well. There are certain situations in your life where you will need to provide the original documents. They are costly to replace.

It is possible to distinguish between copies and original documents by the use of seals with raised seals, colored papers signatures in color and so on. If you're only keeping copies but not originals, you don't need to keep the original document. Be sure to scan it and ensure that the file you scanned is saved.

If you come across passports, make sure they are safe also. Do not keep passports that are expired until they're replaced by an updated one.

Legal documents to keep an eye on include wills, powers of attorneys business licenses, documents proving the formation of a business stocks certificates, patents vehicles, title deeds real estate deeds and transactions, as well as other papers relevant to legal systems.

Also, differentiate the difference between authentic documents as well as copies. Documents with original signatures, sealed seals raised by notary etc. must be kept when you scan copies. They are typically wills, powers-of-advocacy and stock certificates. Other papers that are associated with legal or residential transactions may be duplicates or created from a digital file in the first place. They are acceptable to discard after you've scan copies of them to them in your folders of digital files.

Once you're finished with your paper, it will likely be a tiny pile that will fit into a bank's safe deposit box or even a small fireproof safe or even a simple three-ring binder. If you are using a 3-ring binder, do not punch holes into your important records. Place them in plastic sleeves with the holes punched.

Best Practice Best Practice: My passports are kept in my home, however I have an emergency deposit box to keep the original vital records as well as legal documents. I also scan my documents and save copies to the form of a Dropbox account to be able access to them while traveling. In addition, I keep documents on paper (not copies) in a binder with three rings to ensure that I am able be able to communicate on my own and require someone to gain access to the records.

CATEGORY 2: Medical Records

As a doctor in an office for medical professionals I am very conscient that the healthcare profession isn't up to date in terms of running without paper.

There are a lot of medical centers that handle medical records on a secure online platform. It could be anything from bills to xrays. However, on the flipside there are still companies that have clipboards that can be carried around and make everything written on paper.

Also, it is important to note that, even though the doctor's office has no paper however, they might still want to hand you a piece of paper that you can bring home. This could serve as proof that they reviewed certain notes to you or it could be useful in the event that you're given instructions in case you're not feeling well and you don't know the directions or how to login to view the doctor's notes online in the future.

If you're (or were) in school, there are likely to be some vaccine records too. The records you have on hand could be beneficial throughout your education and may be required in certain fields of work. Certain States have an on-line vaccination database, however this differs between states and could be incomplete if a doctor does not take part in the process of updating the database.

In addition to the history of immunization, I have found two reasons to preserve documents from medical professionals.

The primary reason is to maintain the history of expenses to use to be able to deduct income tax and to help you if you're looking for an insurance or medical billing mistake.

Another reason is to keep an medical history for every person in the family for continuity of health care or for creating a new medical history for life insurance or similar health insurance application.

So, you could consider that you don't have to take pictures of older medical bills that are paid and don't make you eligible for an exemption from tax. It could be a good idea to make the rule that when you find medical bills that are older than a specific date then you can take right to the shredder.

If the paper record includes a the history of a medical procedure, you might still be interested in scanning it even if it's quite old. Keep this in mind: the majority of health insurance or life insurance applications will generally ask questions that pertain to "the past 5 years" or "the past 10 years". You are unlikely to will be required to list the date of an operation that occurred longer than 10 years ago.

If not, at some point in your life, you might have to write down your most recent medical information. It could be to support the application of a life insurance policy, an insurance claim or something uncertain. Documents that you've scanned from your office visits can help you recall the dates of service. If the sole record you that was created is digital (not paper) it is possible to save those files into your digital file directory when they happen.

As you create your digital file folders to store medical records, you could make individual groups for every one of the past 5 years. Then, create a sixth folder which contains all records older than five years ago.

Each person's situation is unique So, make sure you have a system that is appropriate for your needs. Consider that in many instances, the more dated the document is more likely you'll require it and lets you be more flexible when expanding your directories for files.

The best practice is to keep copies of your vaccination records in a distinct digital folder, separate from other records because they are the most frequent records you'll need access to in the near future. Medical bills as well as records from office visits are able to be scanned into separate folders. I suggest creating a separate digital file for every calendar year however, if you have papers that date back more than 10 years, you should put all the old stuff into one folder. E.g. "2010 and before" could be a single folder.

3. FINANCIAL RELEVANCIES

If you've been saving paper throughout your adulthood A lot includes bank statements or utility bills, pay statements, and papers similar to these. Also, you'll possess income tax return as well as the backups that accompany them.

Let's discuss taxes on income first.

Files of income tax

There are a variety of opinions on how long you should keep copies tax returns for income and supporting documents. In general, in the United States the IRS may start a tax audit as early as three years after filing, however, if they determine an issue, they could extend the time period to 7 years, or indefinitely if there is suspicion that income was not reported by more than 25.

In my home, when I switched to a paper-free system I shredded all tax records older than seven years.

Everything else is scanned and then placed into an additional digital folder every year. For anything older than three years, I'd put it all in a pile and then scan it as an individual PDF. For tax returns from the three years most recently it is possible to create subfolders to store copies of the income and copies of tax returns and copies of expenses and donation receipts, copies and so on. At at a minimum, I'd create this type of subfolder for the current tax year, and for the year currently in development.

The reason I would recommend a subfolder system be used for the final tax year that is completed is because it's possible that you will be required to use a document from the year. It could be that you're applying for an loan and the lender will require either the W-2 for last year's tax year or the previous tax year's Federal taxes. It's helpful to have these documents scanned separately and uploaded with your loan application. This is with no additional backups that the bank won't require.

When you go through your papers you will likely find a piece of paper you are certain you'll need to complete your tax return for the year in question. Your accountant will be grateful by allowing you to create subfolders for the current tax year right now. For instance the structure of your files could include a folder titled "2021" and it includes three subfolders "income", "deduction receipts" and "donation receipts". Personal circumstances may require additional folders, make sure you do what's most important to you.

Paycheck stubs, in the event that they exist (most firms don't even offer pay stubs in paper nowadays) they are only kept indefinitely until you receive your W-2. The W-2 is an account of all paycheck stubs. Therefore, it's not necessary to keep them until that point. Scan and shred the paycheck stubs older than last year. Scanne and shred any pay Stubs from the current fiscal year.

Best Practice: Create separate digital folders for the previous 7 tax years. Scanning all tax returns and supporting documents and place the files that you have scanned into the appropriate year's folder. When you scan your return from last year make sure to keep a duplicate of your completed tax return as well as a digital duplicate of your earnings (W-2 1099, W-2) separated from the other backup. Create subfolders that are more precise for the tax year in which you are currently to make your accountant's work simpler. Once you're done scanning, you can shred the papers. It's up to you whether or not to scan tax returns older than seven years, but it's highly unlikely that you'll ever require them.

Bank Statements, credit card bills, loan documents

All of your banking accounts are online and there is no have to keep any papers associated with active accounts. I would never even attempt to scan it. You can just cut it up. The only exception I'd recommend is if you're aware that your tax accountant may require an account statement from a bank or the credit card billing statement due to a reason. You might want to scan the paper into your tax-related income folder right today. You could also download all of your electronic statements from the website of your bank all at tax time. Whichever option is more convenient for you.

If you come across documents that relate to inactive or closed bank accounts, look over the last statement or the most current statement you can locate. Be aware of the account numbers. This is the place where you could discover a bank account you didn't know about.

I often hear that it is necessary to keep bank statements in a safe place because they contain accounts numbers or any other identifying data on the statements. But that is no longer true. The bank statements of today do not contain the entire account number to protect your account. Be sure to know where to locate your complete account number. It's often not displayed when you log into your account on the internet. You need to visit a particular part of the website to find the account number. I would recommend keeping your complete bank account number inside your password manager as they're much more easily accessible.

Best Practice Best practice: Discard (without scan) bank statements for accounts that are active, since the digital documents are already accessible at your bank. If you have a closed bank account look up the latest statement you locate. Make note of account numbers inside your personal password management system.

Cell phone and utility bills

If you have bill for your utility or mobile phone bill for current accounts I would recommend scanning every bill that you own that are current for your calendar. The service provider might have digital copies available online, but you might want to confirm first. It will cut down when scanning.

The reason I would recommend not putting the year in a single statement and not making a single tax return, is due to the possibility that you can claim these expenses as a business expense or the cost of a home office. Particularly when I write this article in the year 2020, many people started the year not expecting to have an office at home towards the time the year was over. If you have already taken deductions for utilities as an expenses for your office, are aware that you must save them on your tax-related income documents.

If you have paper telephone or utility bills from accounts which are no longer being used (especially connected to previous residences) I would suggest scanning a bill for every one of these accounts. This is another aspect which rarely, but occasionally results in the finding of cash.

In the US each state has a law on unclaimed property. Rebates, refunds and overpayments, pay checks which were not collected or refunded, etc. are required to be handed into the state after a specified amount of time, which is usually three years. The state must then look for the person who owns the money. It is possible to use an internet browser and look up your state and "unclaimed properties" to locate the state treasurer's site for this topic. Most of the time, you'll be able to type your name (or the name of a deceased loved one) and determine whether the state has funds that is yours. If they have funds that belong to you The following step will be to establish that you're you. It is often necessary to come with a utility invoice that was issued a while back, in order to prove that you really were the person who lived on XYZ Street and never cashed the rebates that were mailed to you. A utility bill being required as proof of residence may sound like an old-fashioned practice however, I'm speaking from personal the experience of recently collecting old, unclaimed property.

Best practice: Check if your utility company has digital copies of your bills available on the internet (most have). If they do, you are able to take the paper off without scanning. You can scan a copy of the old utility bills from a previous residenceto use as proof of residency.

Your mortgage or lease for your apartment

If you lease your home then you should scan your lease papers or rental agreement as well as any other documents that were started when you first moved into the property.

If you have mortgaged your home, you are able to scan all the papers in connection with it also. If you bought your house within the last 5-10 years , then it's possible that all the papers were given to you electronically.

Best Practice: Scan your mortgage or rental agreement documents and shred them. The digital copy will be just as great just as your original.

CATEGORY 4: THINGS YOU OWN
User manuals

Your storage cabinet may contain many manuals for users.

It is possible to throw all of them into the recycling bin. The entire collection is accessible on the internet. If the thought of throwing away the user's manual causes you anxiety, make sure you ensure that you locate it on the internet. Throw it away.

In my house, I make some exceptions to the manuals included with my home when I purchased it. They left original blueprints, instructions which came with large appliances (like the furnace and sump pump) and the details for the work they contracted to do (replacing roofing). The entire pile of paper is placed in the zippered plastic bag was left inside a kitchen cabinet. I put it there as well. I believe it would be helpful to potential buyers of my house or even an option to sell my house if you ever want to market your house. I haven't actually read the guides however, they were useful to myself as I was a home owner to learn that I owned these items.

Potential buyers of your home do not require instructions for appliances like your oven, dishwasher or microwave. The serial numbers and make/model are on the door, and the manual is available on the internet.

Best Practice: Throw away all manuals for users, except for those that may be useful to a potential buyer of your house.

Warranties

The next step are warranties. If you take the time to go over the fine print of these, then you're likely to have plenty of warranties-related paperwork which have run out. It is possible to put the paper in the recycling bin or in the shredder.

If the warranty has not expired, prior to scanning the document, you might need to review it to determine if you (a) believe there are all documents required to submit an claim, in the event that you need to (b) consider that the conditions and terms are fair (e.g. are they asking you to pay for shipping of $100 for the warranty on an item which costs $20?) or (c) think that you could never ever make use of the warranty. Certain purchases are covered by warranties, however if they're an item costing $20, it's likely that it's not worthwhile to take advantage of the warranty.

Do not waste a lot of time working on this. I will ask myself the questions above and if I consider maybe "maybe ..." then I scan the warranty form and store the document in my electronic file called Warranties. In most cases, you'll need to scan a copy the receipt as well as the warranty details.

BEST practice: Scan all warranties that meet the criteria discussed above.

Your car, as well as the other vehicles

Create a digital file section for every one of your existing vehicles. When you find receipts and purchase documents, as well as maintenance records take a picture of them all and save them in the correct folder. After that, you can dispose of the paper and throw it away.

Keep in mind that if you come across car titles, don't toss them away. The titles of vehicles should be kept alongside important records as well as any other documents that are legal.

What is the procedure for submitting insurance documents to your car? My insurance company provides me with lots of papers. There are likely to be policies, bills and other documents. You should scan the most current bill as well as the most current policy for each car, but the rest will be obsolete or outdated and you'll be able remove it from your home without scanning. Take a picture of any documents that is related to insurance claims.

If you discover papers related to vehicles that you no longer own take a picture of the invoice of sale, or the donation invoice to serve as evidence that you no more have the vehicle. Paper that is not related to cars goes straight to the recycle or shredder bin, and not be scanned.

Best Practice: Keep Original Vehicle Titles. If you own a vehicle you can scan your purchase and maintenance records as well as the most recent insurance documentation. For any vehicle you no longer own, scan evidence that you no anymore the owner.
Your pets

Create a digital file folder for all your pets currently. You can use this folder to save the veterinary records and any other information you may need to keep in the future.

If you come across papers that relate to pets that you no longer own It is unlikely that you have to save or scan the paper in any way.

The best practice is to scan the veterinary records, license information and more. Only for pets that are currently in the care of.
Your home

I've previously discussed salvaging real estate deeds and evidence of transactions in real estate and mortgage terms and lease agreements for apartments and other rental properties.

Look for other documents that are associated with your house, like tax records for your home, maintenance records, service receipts home improvement records, as well as appliance receipts. Take these documents to the scanner in case you have to recall who you worked for or where you purchased an appliance from, or in case you require documentation of the changes made to your house for the purpose of valuing your home.

Best Practice: Scan documents that affect property taxes, valuation of property and other documents connected to your home you may require or need to keep in the future.
Other receipts

Receipts for purchases do not require scanning or stored for any period of time.

Find receipts on a scanner during the current tax year to determine if the item could be tax-deductible.

If you discover the receipts are not more than 90 days old you should review them immediately to determine whether there are items you plan to return or submit to receive the chance to receive a rebate. Ninety days is a good rule of thumb, but store/rebate policies differ. If you discover receipts of this kind keep them in a safe place alongside your documents that require immediate actions.

If, however, you come across an old receipt that isn't tax-deductible that is not for a service or product that is covered by warranty, the chances are high that you'll be able to eliminate it without taking it to scan. Be a bit more naive about this.

If you discover receipts for items tax-deductible from prior tax years, and the receipts aren't included in the tax forms, attempt to determine if they were included on the tax returns or not. If the receipt is of an enormous value in dollars it is possible to think about changing taxes. Scanning those receipts and storing them in the digital file to file your income tax return for the year.

The receipts from older items which aren't tax-deductible, and don't have anything to do with your house, could be thrown away immediately. Remember, follow your gut on this.

Best Practice: Save the original receipts of rebates you intend to submit as soon as possible. Check receipts for tax-deductible purchases and warranties. Throw away any old receipts that you discover.

CATEGORY 3 3. RELEASE MATERIAL

Paper that was backed up with information that can be referenced in the future. This includes things like pages ripped from magazines and recipes, flyers to local events business cards and calendars of events and the latest club directories.

In general, all of these are available online. It is possible that you kept the document because you were concerned that you would lose the details or might not quickly find it. Perhaps, you've subconsciously decided that the moment someone decided it was significant enough to print the details and hand you the paper, it was essential enough to keep. Perhaps you thought it was a shame for you to throw it away even though at some point you knew that the paper was of no use to you.

Some time ago, I purchased an expensive digital product. I didn't purchase it on the internet instead, I purchased it at an event in person and bought it directly from a salesperson. After I made the purchase, the salesperson handed me a small folder with documents that were printed about my brand new item.

He told me "All of this information is available located on our web site, or sent to you via email. We'll give you this file to make you feel as if you're receiving something tangible in exchange for what you pay."

It was refreshingly honest! In telling me this truth the salesman opened my eyes to the same truths on other forms of paper that make its way into my house. The majority of papers are created because it was used to be the norm to produce it but not because it's necessary in the 21st century.

Understanding this will help you examine your reference document in a fresh way. As you come across recipes, flyers, etc. you'll soon realize you can cut down on time and energy by simply throwing away the flyers and other papers.

If you do would like to scan your paper for archive purposes Here are some options. It is already known that you can utilize your scanner to save page to the digital directory of files in your personal computer. One other option I like to use with this kind of material is to save it into an JPG file (or simply snap a picture using my smartphone) then upload the image to Pinterest.

There are already Pinterest boards that are filled with ideas for crafting, recipes as well as travel inspiration. So when I was sifting through my paper and found these types of pages I'd cut off of magazine pages, it was most efficiently for me save the pages to Pinterest. In other words, I'd have ideas for crafting in two places - some on Pinterest and others on my laptop. I needed to be more efficient in my filing.

Another option that's great for magazines is to convert them into JPG and then upload them into Evernote. Evernote incorporates OCR to your documents, so that the JPGs can be searched. This is for me, it means that my scanned magazines are more valuable to me than the paper I need to manually sort through every whenever I'm searching for something.

When you think of magazines, you'll notice that I only talked about using magazines to tear up articles. What happens to magazines you've read, or piles of magazines that you haven't had the pleasure of reading?

I wouldn't suggest scanning all magazines "just in the event of". Many newsstand magazines are consumable, just similar to a printed newspaper. They are designed to be read, and later taken away. The publisher assumes that they will be discarded within a short time. This is why the prices for cover are cheap, the content tends to be monotonous and the majority of the content in magazines are advertisements.

The other kinds of magazines look more similar to books. They could be referred to as print journalsinstead of magazines. They usually don't have ads and thus come with a higher cost. In some instances (though this is not the case all of the time) this implies that the articles aren't repetitive and the entire collection is designed to serve as a reference source.

I've seen on reality TV shows that many people have a difficult to let go of their magazines. It could be the case for you too. However, if you're reading this book , it is likely that you're keen on getting rid of clutter that is not pleasing to the eye.

My personal advice is to get rid of any newsstand magazine. The information in them is likely to come back. You can put them in the recycling bin, or perhaps you can give them away to a homeless shelter or a different community center. It is possible to start with a new magazine if you like magazines, or discover that now isn't the best time to be reading magazines.

If you own magazines or other publications that are ad-free Ask yourself these questions. Do you regularly read them, or have a date when you are certain you use them in the near future? If not then either donate them to charity and recycle them.

If yes, consider whether it would be better to have a digital version of the journal would be beneficial, particularly in the event that it could be searched. A lot of these journals have an archive that is searchable, with an additional cost and, naturally. You should consider whether subscribing the digital archive could be an ideal replacement or supplement to the paper versions that the publication.

I have issues from three journals. Of these there is one that is accessible in digital format but I haven't made the decision to purchase it yet. In the event that I do, I'd gain around two linear feet space on my bookshelf. It is technically possible to make them digital (for my own personal use only) however, this is a long-term commitment in the front of a scanner.

The other two journals in my collection aren't accessible digitally, and since I read them and use them they are treated as books and placed on my shelves.

I hope these ideas will provide you with some thoughts on how to deal with the clutter of your magazines.

The remaining reference papers could be provided by clubs, schools or a church. If the paper isn't urgent action items (category 7) Then consider whether the paper was provided to you as a gesture of courtesy or by custom, and if can be found online.

The best practice is to are a paper-based material owner which contains information that has been duplicated online you can simply dispose of it without scanning. Take a picture of anything that you aren't at ease throwing away immediately however once you've gotten your digital copy the paper copy is tossed to the recycling bin. If you're using Pinterest think about posting JPG scans of the Pinterest boards. Think about using Evernote to search for information ideal for saving magazines. Create rules for yourself regarding what you'll do with any full magazines you discover in the future, whether they are read or not.

CATEGORY 6 PHOTOS and PAPER MEMORIES

Generations younger than us may lack as numerous photographs or paper-based memories, but the majority of us possess memorabilia from the advent of the internet. Tickets stubs, loose photographs album, theatre programs, birthday cards, for instance.

I owned many boxes of these items and enjoyed collecting them, but as time was going on, they began becoming too big. I experimented with different ways of display and storage so that I could be able to enjoy my papers. I created albums and scrapbooks to store some papers while other papers were placed in shadowbox frames in the living room. However, these proved to be temporary solutions , and eventually , the memories of paper were too big to fit in.

The year 2011, when I began creating annual albums of digital photos for my family photographs. I utilize Shutterfly.com to create these albums. After I've completed the album digitally I purchase a print of the album to put on my bookshelf. The albums for printing come in a variety of sizes. I usually choose one that's 12 inches in size. Depending on the amount of photos I upload and the kind of paper I request Shutterfly to use for printing, my final album is between a half-inch to one-inch thick. This is a lot smaller than the scrapbook or photo album that is traditional. I have ten years of photos and stories in albums that are only 6 inches of my shelves.

In the course of time, it became apparent to me the possibility that photo albums weren't limited to photos I uploaded to my smartphone or DSLR camera. I could even scan my old memories of paper into JPGs and upload them to Shutterfly too. Tickets stubs, birthday invitations, birthday cards and other memories from events can be scanned to go into our yearbook of the family.

Utilizing the same technique using the same method, you can create digital scrapbooks using your old papers. You can create themed books by combining all your ticket stubs or birthday cards, in the order that you received them. If you've got a lot of photos from one event, you could scan everything independently or use an image of flatlay. Flatlays are the process of laying everything in a single flat area and then snap the photo from above , taking a birds-eye perspective.

My experience in creating digital albums has been primarily using Shutterfly and I have found the site has advantages and disadvantages.

Benefits of creating memories albums using Shutterfly:

It's absolutely free to store your images on Shutterfly.

* Photos are saved in full resolution.

* They will never delete your images - there is no need to purchase an annual subscription or something similar. (Note this has been their policies for years However, as with any company which offers the service at no cost it is possible to alter the terms of service at any point.)

If you create an album of photos on Shutterfly it's possible to think of that it is backed up. In other words, if you bought an album in physical form and it was destroyed by fire, Shutterfly still has a backup.

It's simple to use and new features are constantly added.

Then, in 2020 they started offering the option of designing your book for absolutely no cost. All you need to do is to mark your top images, and they will include them in the books in a sensible way. I tried the feature, and found it awesome!

* Shutterfly often offers coupon codes for FREE 20-page books that are 8x8 inches in size. I've used these before and they're perfect for small albums of artwork by children or gifts for grandparents or images of a vacation.

The cons of creating memories albums using Shutterfly:

* They're expensive If you're trying to fit the entire year's worth memories and photos into a 12x12-sized book. I'm spending about $100 for an annual yearbook that way and that's only when the website offers 50 percent off (which most of the time is). You can also make use of coupons to get free 8x8 books with up to 20 pages.

CATEGORY 7 CATEGORY 7: AFFECTIVE PAPER

The final category of paper you'll see is the one that you can take action on. It is likely to be the smallest stack of papers. The papers you hang on to since you want to get them out of your system as soon as possible. Formulas to fill out for your child's school, coupons that you're planning to use shortly and party invitations you need to reply to and bills to pay These are just a few examples of these papers.

There is no reason to digitize the paper prior to when you've acted upon it. However, it requires a place to live. A lot of people the home is in side of the fridge or even on high of the kitchen table. If this is what you prefer it's acceptable. I prefer a vertical "in" tray that sits on my desk near my computer. It's also possible to put the paper in front of my laptop so that I'm more motivated to take action on it , and later get it off my desk.

The most important thing to do when dealing with a paper that is actionable is to establish a procedure to review it regularly. This could be every day like the moment you return from work and are taking care of your mail. It could be that cleaning out the "in" tray every week is sufficient. Once you've made a decision on the document, you are able to scan it (only should you need to) and throw it away.

****
***

These are the seven categories of papers you'll discover at home. Next chapter I'll discuss the same categories, but as if you were another's house or you've received paper that you must sort. If none of that applies to you, the situation, skip ahead in chapter seven in which I'll provide tips for how to maintain your paper-free office for the future.

Guidelines for filers that been given papers
This chapter is specifically geared towards those who inherit papers from parents or relative, or who are forced to sort out paper they don't know about.

I've observed that many people open their eyes to clutter in their paper when they are caregivers for somebody else. The paper we use isn't an issue however theirs is. How do we handle this paper if we do not know what's going on?

Let me first bring up a few subjects that have been covered in earlier chapters. Do not make a decision to declare "paper bankruptcy" (chapter one) be aware of yourself and your timetable (chapter one) and create an action plan to deal with stress (chapter five).

The timeline might be shorter and more hectic in the case of documents from an older relative. It's understandably difficult, but I suggest getting the papers organized as quickly as you can , and best in the time your relative is living.

We'll now look at strategies to deal with paper, even if that paper was not created by you. In the previous chapter , I defined seven different categories. My last classification being "actionable" papers like documents to sign, lists of tasks as well as other forms of paper. This category may not pertain to your family member therefore in this chapter, we'll look at only six types of paper.

CATEGORY 1: VITAL RECORDS AND LEGAL DOCUMENTS

In the previous chapter , I covered important documents and records and explained why in the majority of situations you should not need to eliminate the original documents.

It is the same for the original vital documents (birth, divorce, marriage, or death certificates) even if the person who signed the document is dead. It's obvious with regards to the death certificate. You might be thinking that, if a person has passed away, they won't require a birth certificate again. It is still recommended to keep it for the sake of family history. Vital records are those that show that a particular individual is related to another. These kinds of documents become increasingly difficult to replace when the person isn't alive to make the request. If you're extremely limited in storage space, scans of marriage and birth certificates are acceptable to preserve family history. I'd recommend keeping original death certificates in the event that the deceased person has recently passed away. The original document is likely to have the seal or watermark which signifies it's not a duplicate. It is possible that the original document may be required by probate courts or in any other legal system. It is essential to have one replica of the certificate of death in your possession since the estate of your loved one is being resolved.

It is also important to search for legal documents, such as wills, powers of attorneys medical advance directives divorce settlement agreements life insurance policies business licenses and proof of business incorporation Stock certificates, patents and vehicle titles as well as real estate deeds and transactions, and any other documents that are related to law enforcement. If you're settling an estate, you'll need these documents.

If your loved one has passed away You can search for documents referred to as Letters Testamentary, Letters of Administration and Letters of Representation (the names differ between states). The document was issued by a probate court and lists the people who have the authority to be appointed on behalf of the deceased. If you've been given the document, it's probably you, but it could also be your step-parent or sibling.

It is also important to note that if you don't locate any of these kinds of documents, and you're taking care of an aged relative, you may require assistance from your family member and trusted experts to get these documents put in place as quickly as is possible.

The medical advance directive can also be known as a living trust which outlines the procedures that are both desired and unwelcome and allows the appointing of two or three individuals who can make medical decisions in the event that the person signing the directive becomes incapacitated. Make sure that your loved one completes this as quickly as is possible and make it available to present to your loved one's doctor and bring to the hospital in the event that your loved one is admitted to the hospital.

If you cannot discover an original will (or the name of the estate lawyer to verify the existence of an estate plan) You can ask your relative for the wishes of his or her relatives for the estate funeral arrangements, funeral arrangements, organ donation or burial or cremation. Start the process of helping your relative write the will. There will be a charge however it's a crucial document to have. Simple wills can be done in 20 minutes online here: https://www.daveramsey.com/recommends/will

Best Practice: Scan and save all original vital records you find. Save and scan all legal documents that may need to be presented in the probate courts to resolve the loved ones' estate. If you're looking after someone who is living and you don't have the will or medical advance directive then stop your work and ensure that they are completed before you do any other activities.

CATEGORY 2: Medical Records

The scans of the medical record are as effective as the original documents. So it is a matter of whether it is worth scanning to begin with.

This type of paper might make you feel anxious. If this is the case, it's the perfect time to call someone else to help so that you don't have to examine the papers.

Caregiver of living relatives are likely to take a scan of at least couple of years worth of records to ensure that they continue care. At a minimum, you should scan at least one record for each name of the provider (doctor) which you locate. The future doctors or caregivers of your loved ones are able to request the histories of prior doctors however only if they are aware of the names of those doctors. If you scan documents that have various providers, you'll always have the records of the names.

However there are some providers who are not as attentive or prompt with responses to inquiries for medical records as one would like and they do end their services or retire at times. If you are having any concerns about keeping a medical record for your relative then you can opt to go through every medical record that you can find. It is also possible to select an exact date and only scan documents that were created within the time frame, for instance the last 10 years.

Medical expenses may be tax-deductible, so make sure you check them also. If you're not familiar with your relatives' income tax returns, and your relative has suffered significant medical expenses, you are able to scan any bills that you discover to discuss with your tax advisor later.

If you've inherited papers from a deceased loved one scan medical bills to get tax records remains a possibility. The relative might still have to complete a tax return or other medical expense that is significant may be tax-deductible.

There is a lower chance you'd need to retain the medical history of the deceased in the event of a possibility of a lawsuit which the medical record is considered to be evidence.

The best practice is to consider the individual circumstances of your loved one and set rules about the kinds of documents and the ages of the documents you'll scan. If you are having trouble making a decision, keep in mind that you have the option of scanning any medical records you discover. It is possible to categorize the records according to the name of the doctor.

Chapter 3: FINANCIAL RELEVANCIES

If you've inherited papers from an older family member, most of it will include utility bills, bank statements or pay stubs for the paycheck, as well as other papers of this kind. Also, you will find income tax returns as well as the backups for them as well.

Like I did earlier in this chapter, we'll discuss the tax returns for income first.

Disclaimer: I'm not an accountant. I do not offer tax advice. Instead, seek the most up-to-date guidance from a tax attorney. Remember that you have the option of scanning every piece of paper.
Files of income tax

Determine whether your loved one hired an accountant for tax preparation to prepare their annual tax returns or if they self-prepared. Most likely, you can determine this by reviewing the signature page of Form 1040 (or similar cover pages) and checking if the tax preparer's name is mentioned. Is the tax preparer still operating? How likely is it they will remain in business for the next seven years? Are they authorized to communicate with authorities at the IRS for your family member? Do they have all the copies of your relatives' tax returns and all of the backup documentation and calculation? Do they have any digital copies that they are able to give to you? Answering these inquiries can assist you in deciding the best strategy for scanning.

If you live in the United States, the IRS could initiate a tax audit within three years of filing. However, in the event of a finding of cause, they could go back in the seven year period of limitations. So, it is possible to save scanned copies of your previous 3 tax returns or the last 7 years. I would recommend scanning it all in one document since it is unlikely that you will have to revisit it. Anything older than seven years could be destroyed without scanning.

If you are unable to discover evidence from the last 3-7 years of tax return It could be a cause for concern. Find out whether your relative submitted the tax returns in time.

You can request transcripts of relatives' tax returns from the deceased to verify that they're still valid. Read more about the process on the IRS website here: https://www.irs.gov/businesses/small-businesses-self-employed/deceased-taxpayers-getting-information-from-the-irs

If your loved one is recently deceased, they probably is required to complete a tax return for the final year. You should take a look at any documents that you encounter which pertain to expenses and income for the year in which your relative has to file.

BEST WAY: Create separate digital file folders to store the last 7 tax years. Take a picture of all tax returns and documents supporting them and then put all scanned documents in the appropriate folder for the year. Check if your relative is an accountant for tax purposes who can be able to assist IRS IRS in the case that they were to be audited.

Bank Statements, credit card bills, loan documents

When you're dealing with bank records of a living relative, take them in the same manner as you would treat your own paper , as described in chapter 5. Check bank account number and ensure that you are able to access the electronic files for the benefit of your family member. As long as you're able cut and take the bank statements off the paper. If you're unable to access the bank statements online for your loved ones and you are unable to scan the documents you can find. Create separate digital file folders to each bank account, and distinct sub-folders for every calendar year. Each year should comprise only 12 documents at the most.

If you've received many papers from a deceased relative , and you're not aware of the bank accounts, organize the paper according to the bank account, and then go through the last three years of each bank account. This will ensure that you are ready for the possibility that you are subject to the possibility of an IRS tax audit that goes further than 3 years.

If you've inherited bank records that date back more than three years, they're safe to destroy however, only after having examined accounts' numbers as well as figured out whether the accounts are still in existence or not. It is one of those situations where unexpected cash is discovered due to an account that has been closed that nobody remembered.

BEST WAY TO USE IT Best Practice: Sort the paper by account number, and confirm that the account is in good standing, closed active/inactive. Download, or scan, from the bank the last three years of the paper to be used for tax audits. Note down any steps you have to do to close the account or hand them over to another person.

Cell phone and utility bills

The same guidelines from chapter 5 is applicable to utility bills for your relative. Take a picture of any bill of the tax year in which you are currently that could help for your tax return. For older bills, you should make sure you scan each one of the relatives' previous addresses. They will be used as proof of residency when they are required in accordance with the law on unclaimed property. Check out chapter 5 for further details on this topic.

Other utility bills are able to be shredded without scanning.

Best practice: Take a original utility bill from a previous home, to prove residency. Take a picture of bill for utilities from current tax year , if they're tax-deductible.
The mortgage of your relative or the apartment lease

The same guidelines from chapter 5 can be applied to the mortgage of your living relative or lease agreement. If you have an elderly relative who is a homeowner ensure that you have a plan of what happens to the property and mortgage when he/she dies. Mortgage payments have to be continued to prevent the possibility of foreclosure.

Executors of wills is entrusted with certain rights that other members of the family are not able to exercise Therefore, you must are aware of where the will of your relative is .

If your loved one has passed away the mortgage or lease will be taken care of during the finalization of the estate. It could at present be null and null. Take a picture of any evidence of prior property transactions.

BEST WAY: Scan the rental agreement or mortgage documents and then shred the original documents. Digital copies are as great just as the real thing.

Category 4: PAPER TO STUFF THEIR OWNERS' RELATED

The same advice in chapter 5 is applicable to this type of. If you've inherited your family member's papers, then you are likely to find that the relative is either downsizing or has died and has no use for their "stuff". This could be a straightforward kind of papers to sort out since the majority of it can be recycled.

User manuals don't need to be kept or scanned and can be recycled immediately.

The warranty information may be outdated and insignificant to you. Make sure to scan any warranties that relate to recent purchases where you have a good understanding of the item and are willing to adhere to the warranty conditions and terms should they be required.

Does your relative have an automobile? If not, take a picture of any documentation of car donation or sales you can find, and then throw away any other paperwork associated with the car. If the relative of yours owns an automobile, follow the same guidelines as described in chapter 5.

Do your relatives have pets? Check veterinary records, license information etc. For current pets only.

Do you know if your relative has property, such as a house or estate? Take a look at documents related to property taxes, valuation of property and other information that is related to the property (such in service certificates) you may need or need to recall in the future.

If you find random receipts, you should only scan them when they're recent and could be tax-deductible. In other cases, discard them.

CATEGORY 5 CATEGORY 5: RELEASE MATERIAL

This is the easiest category to deal with since this kind of paper belongs to someone else, but not to you. There is no need to keep any of these recipes, magazine articles and so on. They are fine to get rid of without scanning.

CATEGORY 6 PHOTOS as well as paper memories

This is one of the more challenging categories due to a variety of reasons. Photos of your relatives and souvenirs could be a source of inspiration for you too. There could be lots of photos and scrapbooks to look through. The paper could be fragile.

If your relative is living, you can ask for their assistance in ensuring the people in the pictures are identified. It's extremely disappointing to find a collection filled with photos of people who you don't know and not be able to determine who they are.

In other words, treat this kind of paper the same way as your own photographs and memories. I suggest digitizing these memories even if you opt not to save the albums. Digital copies be a backup in the event of loss caused by decay or fire, and you can easily share them with others in your family.

If the job seems overwhelming You can ask someone else to scan the albums on your behalf or stay with you during your time of work. Read chapter 5 for suggestions on how to create digital albums.

Chapter 4: Keeping the paper-free office for the foreseeable future

Congratulations! Your old paper has been scanning, and you now have the digital file directory within your PC. Now, what do you do with the paper that is coming in? Consider if it is necessary to look it up again and then scan it and then save the digital file into the appropriate file folder.

Make a decision

If you are the first to feel a sheet of paper determine right away if you truly need it or can throw it away (recycle) it and not revisiting it. If it's not going to the recycling bin, it's considered to be a legal paper. It doesn't matter if it's a birthday card , or an invoice for an item that is tax-deductible. Place the paper where you'd like to put your actionable papers and handle it in accordance with your plan. I recommend scanning and reviewing your actionable papers at least every day, or weekly.

Scan

The most efficient timetable for you will be determined by the scanner type you're using as well as the time of the day that you work with the most paper.

We'll first look at the reasons why the scanner type is important. If you own an all-in one scanner and printer as well as a flatbed scanner equipped with ADF is active and ready to go anytime. This is extremely convenient for taking paper from your home as swiftly as possible , without having to handle your paper "later". It is possible to walk your mail straight onto the scanner to then feed it through without thinking about it. Similar to school papers and work papers.

If you're using your smartphone or handheld scanner the scanning of your paper will require a bit more effort. It is necessary to connect your handheld scanner to scan every page. You can also lay the paper out in a suitable lighting and snap photographs of every page. It's only about an hour however it's quite an effort that it may not necessarily be convenient to manage it each occasion it occurs. It's the time to add the document to your"to-do" list.

Paper is typically brought into your home in mail from the post office or school papers or papers brought to work and receipts from the shop. Which one is the most typical for you? My home is the post office and that's why I take a walk to the scanner to sort through my mail inbox. If I do bring home receipts or other piece of paper I'd like to save the paper, it goes into the inbox to be saved for future use.

If I had an portable scanner I used to leave the paper near my computer and then scan it at least once per week. To be precise I don't receive many pieces of mail that's not junk, so I'd scan a couple of pages per week.

For my work (the health office) the scanning schedule differs because handling paper is an integral aspect of my job. When I'm working I scan papers as soon as I've touched it, and then it is sent right into the shredder. When I'm not at the timer, paper resides in the fax machine, or the inbox until

I return to work. The only filing cabinet I have is digital.

That leads to the final next...
File your digital scan

Your scanner transmits your digital image to an overall directory on your personal computer. The phone will store your image or scan in an album general to. You must still move your digital files into their appropriate albums or folders for digital files, so that your birthday cards won't get confused with receipts that are tax-deductible.

This isn't so important as the actual creation of an image, but you can do what you like and fits your style. Make your file directory to allow you to drag and drop your scans to where you want them to be. It's preferential to spend a few seconds to do this immediately as you remember the items you've scanned, however you can also go along with this process every week or even monthly. You can even do it annually if you are not adamant about putting off filing. It is not recommended to do it annually however I have been known to delay and file my taxes monthly.

Sharing your digital file cabinet

The best thing about the physical cabinet for filing is that several people can utilize it. This isn't a good reason to keep the physical cabinet. It is just a matter of getting comfortable with the idea of sharing digital files exactly the same way.
Access to read/write for multiple users

In chapter 3, I advised that Windows users use the Public folder to store their files directory, especially if there are any other users within your home network or smaller company network that require access to the digital file cabinet.

Mac users are able to add additional users to their home using the Users or Groups. Anyone who is permitted to be a part of your Users and Groups is able to join your Mac through the network. You can modify

the user's access as well as shared folder access when needed.
To allow read-only access to other users

If you are using a cloud-based backup service that's real-time like Carbonite it is possible to use your login credentials to other users, granting them read-only access to your online file cabinets.

If you regularly back up your digital file cabinet onto an external drive, or to cloud storage on a computer, then you may give that information to someone you trust. This person would be able to access the backups of the digital cabinet, which could mean that certain files may be obsolete or not available.

You may only wish to share specific files with a specific group of users. For instance, you could share income tax documents to your accountant as well as other kinds of documents that you need for your attorney. In these instances, you should check with each professional to determine their preferences for ongoing file sharing. In the ideal scenario, they'll have an encrypted service safe for the kind of file you're sharing.

Access to the user in the event in an emergencies

If you own the binder that holds the birth certificate of your child, your vehicle title or other documents. You might want to describe the whereabouts of your digital file cabinet and then putting the information into the binder too.

Documents that are essential to have when you cannot be able to speak on your own, like an estate plan or a medical directive, must be passed on to someone you trust, such as a family member or friend.

Chapter 5: Organizing your Mind

This chapter will guide you understand the methods and techniques to keep your mind well-organized. It will also assist you in understanding the guidelines for organizing your mind and the techniques that are used to manage your thoughts.

2.1 Strategies to Rewire minds

The brain is an extremely powerful organ. It can gather and storing information of the world's most advanced supercomputers in world can't. The brain contains around 100 trillion synaptic (synapses) connections that continually relay information to the other parts of your body, brain and.

The most intricate structure on earth can be found in the brain of a human. We're just starting to scratch the surface of understanding this amazing phenomenon, even with the latest technology and measurement equipment.

Though the brain is strong and powerful but it's also prone to the whimsy of thinking. This is mostly an evolutionary consequence, in which the reptile portion of the brain, the amygdala is still producing bizarre impulses and emotions. It is within the amygdala that the reaction to "fight or fight" is activated. Fortunately one of the more advanced (and developed) part of the brain -- the forebrain capable of overriding the wandering thoughts. While it isn't easy initially, there's an incredible way for our brain to instill habit in our minds. In essence, the brain will begin to organize itself into certain patterns.

Here are some suggestions to aid your mind:
1. Do not multitask, Simply:
Human brains are incompetent to multitask. The only thing it can boast about that distinguishes of on many workplaces is that it is completely incoherent. The only thing a brain can do effectively is to talk and breathe. Every task that is at an upper level, such as writing emails and cooking, filing, computing or cooking, etc. is a one-tasker. It's the only real method to organize. Yet the idea is to "multitask," right? In reality, you have plenty of work to complete and that's the only method to do it. I'm sorry for bursting your bubble What you're really doing is shifting your mind's focus on one

thing to the next. Two reasons suggest this behavior is not healthy:

(1) It depletes the brain's resources (1) It drains your brain's resources

(2) The brain is less efficient, and requires longer for the brain to pay its attention on a particular task.

2. Keep A Written List To Organize Your Mind:

Your brain, though an incredible computer is still a limited resource. Making a list of things to accomplish is a good method of freeing up needed brain space.

Human brains are drawn to lists written down. Why? What is the reason? Because lists tap into our innately tuned method by which the brain organises and comprehends information. Indeed the lists have a specific kind that appeals to the brain's tendency to remember things. Lists written down are an excellent method to ease the stress caused by memory loss.

3. Disconnect:

We live in a society that today is Technology obsessed. A few prominent mental health experts consider that for millions of people, addiction to technology is similar to an emotional and chemical dependency like alcohol and drugs.

Continuously overloading your brain with information isn't a good idea, since the brain requires time to think, reflect and refresh itself. Incessant flow of information, either from a laptop or else, can be dangerous and is in direct opposition to the natural brain structure of the human brain.

4. Be mindful:

Another word to mention is mindful. You've likely been exposed to (or have practiced) meditation, mindfulness or both. If you're focused and attentive, great for you... Thank you for your brain. If you've heard about it take a look at becoming a student.

Being mindful is an attitude of living and a way of life. It doesn't matter if you're adopting a regular routine of morning meditation or taking a 3 minute lunch break, this time, you're entitled to. Just pay the attention to your actions without judgment or criticism. The focus is switched to the breath when meditating while your mind wanders then it returns. It's certainly easier to say than to do but it's possible to (and should) practise while you're learning.

Without going into the scientific journaling mode, let's simply declare that mindfulness has remarkable effects on your brain. There are a lot of wonderful things you can find online on the subject of. Mindfulness isn't about clearing the mind focus on only one aspect. Meditation isn't a blunder when people who have their minds wander claim that the brain behaves as if it's a dog that's out of control. The process is about locating it and then resetting it.

5. Put all the stuff in the same Place:

You've probably been given this information at some point. It turns out that there's an explanation for this. The brain there's an area called the hippocampus which is the exact part of the brain which asks a squirrel to tell it to hide its nuts, and operates similar to.

The hippocampus is known as "location memory" This is a term that is appropriate due to the amazing capacity that this brain structure has to connect significant occasions (placing the keys) to specific locations (your fridge).

6. Pauses for breaks:

As we've already mentioned the brain has a finite amount of resources, with one of them being electricity. This is why your brain functions like computer systems The more information that is processed and processed, the more amount of energy used.

Due to this high energy use and the fact that you're not able to sit for long hours at the fast-paced work environment, and keeping the same effectiveness. Thus, breaks are crucial to your mind. Engage in something fun and stimulating to make the most of your time off. Our bodies and brains do not have the capacity to handle long periods of time at work. Although it might seem that a long time in front of your computer is the ideal way to get the work completed, it can be detrimental to your productivity. Research has proven that the most productive work schedule typically lasts for 52 minutes of continuous work, with intervals of 17 minutes. Although this method of systematically arranging your schedule may not be feasible in the majority of cases you can win by simply making sure to take breaks. Be sure to take with a few breaks throughout the every day.

7. Make use of a calendar to organize Your Schedule:

The old calendar you have in your closet may not be suitable however, the usage for a calendar of one way or another is an excellent idea. Calendars are great to help you outsource your memory and clearing memory space in your brain according to neuroscientists.

Therefore, download an application or make use of Outlook or simply download your hands on the "flip" calendar created by an old. It's a good idea to regularly use a calendar and witness your life getting easier and less anxiety-inducing.

8. Use the same password:

There is a need for a password today for almost every item. Create a password by yourself, and test using the same password, or an alternative. Certain applications require that the password be altered for security reasons specifically in workplace. Making a change or adding an image or number is an easy solution to that.

Rememberthat your brain can turn repetitive actions into habits. Utilizing the same password or with a slight modification could make it easier to remember them , while clearing the brain space that is desperately needed.

9. Get enough sleep:

In the 1950s, sleep was a term that was not understood. It was just a matter of knowing that it was getting late, so we grew tired, and then fell in bed until the next day. Researchers today realize that sleep is an essential element of brain functioning. If we don't get enough rest there can be issues with the concentration levels as well as balance, memory and mood.

Research suggests that adults should get at least seven hours of rest. For teenagers (age 14-17) at least eight hoursof sleep, school-age youngsters (6-13) 9 hours and preschoolers (3-5) 10 hours, infants (1-2) for at minimum 11 hours and babies (4-11 months) for at least 12 hours, and newborns at the minimum of 14 hours.

10. Discover Something new:

Neuroscience has taught us about the brain something remarkable: it continues change the way it is formed.

It was thought that the brain began to shrink after the age of a certain point, typically teens. Today, scientists have discovered that throughout all of the existence, your brain's shape and structure changes.

The brain makes connections every time you learn that is any subject. The new connections slowly alter the structure of the active portion of the brain. Researchers refer to this as "neuroplasticity," and its importance goes beyond learning, to areas like the ability to compensate for trauma and diseases.

11. Find the right amount of Percentage Of:

It's easy to lose focus and fall prey to distracting thoughts when the task in hand isn't easy or easy when trying to finish your work. People thrive when they are faced with a challenging task that can cause boredom but isn't too difficult that it causes anxiety due to its simplicity. If you select a task with care and prudence you'll greatly increase your chance of having flow.

12. Be in control of your emotions:
You're in control of how you react to your feelings , however you can't determine how certain things will make you feel. In the first place, you have to be open to yourself about what you are feeling and why you feel that way. The transfer of anger into the actions you desire is much easier. Labelling and identifying your feelings in the moment you feel it is essential. Making connections between the sensations you experience can make the emotion real and less enigmatic. This can help you calm down, figure out what's going on behind the feeling and get on with your life. When you try to control your feelings , without facing them and taking on your task, they could take over your life and impede your focus.

13. Keep Concentration:
We've all experienced the dreadful feeling of sitting down to do something crucial, only to quickly lose focus while we are supposed to get straight into the work. Your brain requires to be allowed to fully immerse into an activity. It takes anywhere from five to twenty minutes for people to focus. If you can get yourself to remain focused on the

task for a period of twenty minutes without all distractions, the chances are better to be able to keep your focus and achieve the state of flow. The best method to achieve this is to remove or turn off all your common distractions (phones and emails, as well as social media, etc.) and pay attention to the time until you've accomplished nothing else but work for at least twenty minutes even though you're not making much progress. When you reach the twenty-minute mark, it's likely that things will begin to cook.

14. Shift Sets

It's best to shift your focus on your goal after taking breaks. Whatever "in in the flow" you were prior to stopping for a break, at times when you're trying to focus on your work, you'll be back at square one. You must reorganize your thoughts following the steps one by making a set change, especially in the event that you're having trouble getting back into work. It is possible to return to flow fast after a break however, this should be done in a controlled manner.

All in all It's not particularly difficult to organise the mind so that it can feel flowing however it takes concentration and discipline.

15. Find the connections

You now know how to manage your stress and focus on one task at a given time and on your agenda. It is possible to get rid of this from distractions. If you require it your memory will be prepared to act. You're flexible and capable of swiftly moving between tasks. To open up new perspectives, ideas, and connections you break and move your body and shift your direction of focus.

The "rules in order" together can help you change not just your habits of attention, but also the way you think about your life. You'll be in control instead of feeling anxious.

You'll be more successful and therefore have more time for exercises that are healthy to your body as well as your mind. You'll feel better about yourself, and well-being is enhanced by positive emotions. You will also be able to apply your focus to the goal of achieving your fitness and health goals.

2.2 Strategies to organize thoughts:
In an ever-growing mess, everything's swirling around, and you can't have any idea how to comprehend the world around you.

There are, of course methods to learn the funniest ideas.

Tips for organizing your thoughts

* Use sticky notes as well as frame.
* Gather a pile of sticky notes, and place them close to a wall or stand. Write one thought down on each sticky note and put the note up to the wall. Keep doing this until you've got many notes. then you can begin separating the notes by hand.

Create the Mind Map

Mind maps are an approach to bring together diverse thoughts. Start by sketching one thought on an article of paper that is at the center. Then, draw an outline of the thought, radiating across the entire length of the page. Add an identical or related thought. Keep adding thoughts onto your maps, making sure that they are linked to one and each other.

Keep Notes on your Index Card:

Index cards are an excellent option to keep track of your thoughts and ideas. If you are thinking of a major idea you could use the top red line , and note similar thoughts below on the lines below or make use of a single card to represent an idea or thought. Shuffle your decks as you search for ways to improve your method to organize and sort information.

Make A List:

Make a note of your thoughts. Write down one thought in an outline, and continue moving until all of your thoughts are recorded at the present time. It is then possible to return and begin separating the list into smaller sections.

Create A Pie Chart:

You've probably seen pie charts in the past. They are maps that have circles (or the pie) shape, shaded by various regions. Note down some of your thoughts. You can then give different proportions of your thoughts or the levels of importance.

Innovative ways to organize your ideas

Write a letter about your feelings:

Turn off your mobile phone, set your computer to bed and relax with the paper you've written on and a pen in your desk. Just pretend to write an email to a person you know. What is the way in which you express your thoughts to them? Spend the time to think and then write the letter.

How to organize various objects What are all those bits and pieces do? Utilizing these suggestions, you can organize different items.

Create A Collage:

Create a collage from your thoughts with photographs and photos from newspapers, magazines, and so on. Lay it out, and then stick it all onto a poster board or sheets of paper. You can create this in digital format too; you can make a collage of images that you like on Pinterest for instance.

Make a Table of Contents:

To write a book, imagine that you're making a table of content. What of your ideas should appear at the beginning of the book? what should be at the conclusion of your thoughts?

Maintain an eye on your Timeline:

The idea of listing your thoughts in a calendar or timeline format will give you a sense of perspective that's desperately required. You can create a calendar that shows the calendar's months and weekdays or the times during the week. In each of the slots, write one thought in each month or every Monday. The idea is to arrange your thoughts in an outline of your thoughts in order of what is first, and what follows and so on.

Write down your thoughts:

Here's a simple method to record what you really think. Use a voice recorder or other device that records voice to capture your thoughts. Set the recording aside for a couple of days after which you can take a look. You'll get a different perspective on what you feel.

Ideas for Organizing Your Thoughts

If you ever feel bored at home, make an effort to take on these productive tasks.

How Do You Brain-Off?

It is helpful to focus on something and not think about it. This could include entering the business card information into a spreadsheet or spreadsheets, ironing clothes or knitting and sewing cleaning furniture, cleaning furniture, filing papers or cleaning your workspace or space. Your mind will sort through your tasks as you work.

Relieve yourself, or sit in peace:
Meditation can help relax your mind and body. It can also assist you to to process your feelings. Make the blinds draw, turn off the lights or dim them, and then sit on the ground or in a chair.

Do not sleep on it:
What is now confusing and confusing in the morning, will appear quite different. If the thoughts that are running through your head aren't able to be coherent, you should go to bed for the night.

A PHYSICAL WAY TO ORGANIZE YOUR feelings

Do some exercise:
Move your body, and pumping your blood. Going to the gym, running about, throwing frisbee or playing catch with a buddy or walking, and making errors. The change in pace can give the mind some time and allow your mind to play in the background of the puzzle you've been working on.

Get Outside In Nature:
Take a walk and enjoy an outdoor experience. You can relax on an outdoor bench or walk along a trail stroll with your dog or take a look around the beautiful

green grassy area. You can get out of your ears and focus on the beauty.

Talk to a person you know or any other member or family member:

It is helpful to discuss things with your partner at times. You'll feel better having something off your head and off your chest. Additionally, your companion will definitely help you discover patterns that you may have missed or help clarify and make clear your thoughts.

Tell a story:

The act of telling a story aloud will prompt you to consider what is important and isn't essential. Therefore, start with your ideas and create the story. "It was a period of time"

Simple steps to boost your Brain Power:

Our brains are arranged mostly, just like human computers. They function in similar ways to a great extent. If we wish to improve our daily productivity it is essential to eliminate of the temporarily stored "data" storage and restart our brains in order to operate at our highest levels.

In other words, we could quickly experience brain overload due to numerous circuits at once and a myriad of programs (thought) that are running in the background that are often "freeze in." This can make us incapable of recollecting all the information or processing information slower as we'd prefer.

It might sound strange It may sound odd, but it is logical when you begin to think about.

You'll significantly increase your ability to focus on your tasks, finish them and reach the goals you set by making it part of your habit to schedule some time each day to organize and clean your brain.

A clear mind is more productive than one that is constantly overloaded.

Additionally, a brain that is overwhelmed can forget important tasks, things or information, as well as deadlines. The productivity rate, too is suffering. We are clearly not able to focus and utilize our brains and talents to their highest potential.

You'll experience greater balance, less stress and more energy as an additional benefit. The constant swirling of thoughts creates a lot of tension and prevent our minds from relaxing. This can cause brain fatigue which causes us to be exhausted and cranky.

It's not that difficult to arrange your thoughts. It's just only a few minutes every day to improve your mind with simple tools. Three easy steps to increase your brainpower.

1. Choose the Most Optimal Time:

The ideal way to do this is best carried out twice a day, starting in the morning, and then after bedtime, however, it's not for everyone.

Pick the time that works for your schedule most. It will perform every time. The trick is to be consistently doing it.

A few people feel that early morning breakfast, coffee and a workout are the first things they need. They believe their brain is waking up. They definitely need an increase in caffeine, an increase in tension, and fuel to make thought patterns that are coherent.

2. Choose Your Logging Method:

All note-taking or productivity apps that you can install for your smartphone will help you record your thoughts and work. You can also use the voice recording option if you like. Even the function of the base note can be used.

A folder or organizing program on your computer could function similarly, for example Outlook, OneNote, or Evernote.

While by nature, some are more of a "techie," They still prefer using a pad and pen to complete the task. The most effective method is the most simple.

Whichever tool you pick ensure that it is easy to use and fast.

3. Quickly dump everything:

You should dump everything you've got in your head, and be sure to check that you have everything... is not just work but also feelings worry, doubts, and thoughts too.

Take them all out. Don't even think about figuring them out to do later. Simply get these thoughts out of your brain to stop them from running around and use your brain's power and energy.

Consider whether you'll have a need or desire to act on any of those issues now, after you've completed.

If yes then add the tasks from your current checklist of to-dos or tasks (do you have any of these rights?).

If you don't know the answer What is the idea? Put it in a notebook of thoughts, a work notebook, or even a paper to be followed up on later.

Are you really referring to an issue you're facing or have concerns about? You can record it in a paper or notebook that you can then think about. (If you don't return to review them then maybe they weren't that crucial!) It's easy. In no more than 5-10 minutes are needed!

A Tiny habit that has great benefits:

You're no longer concerned about your ability to let go of the thoughts and worries that weigh you down. You'll be more adept in relaxing our minds while enjoying other aspects in our daily lives.

You'll fully connect with the the world outside of your while you're not within your head. This is a good thing considering the time it takes from 5-10 minutes.

Every day, an average person thinks 70,000 times that aren't organized. If you're not sure how to manage these thoughts, they have the potential to negatively impact your productivity.

If you give in to the storm of emotions running through your mind your brain becomes chaotic and the more unnecessary thoughts you have the more power you can give them.

Our thoughts are just thoughts, not factual information. When you start being influenced by the negative or distracting thoughts that your inner voice is telling you The momentum that you think about is likely to slow; that's why it's important to arrange your thoughts and your thoughts.

Chapter 6: What is the best way do we begin to Organization in Our Lives?

A lot of people would like their lives to be more organised, but they don't know what to do So here are a few things to think about organizing and ways to deal with each one.

3.1 Organizing your Desk

You can drive at dawn. You have the route down to a science and, in the sleep you can probably take it. Therefore, when issues such as roadblocks, construction, or detours are spotted and you are unable to navigate them, it can be a hassle and deter you from completing the job in a timely manner.

Being in a noisy atmosphere is like driving through the city at the end of a weekday afternoon. there are always some detours, the traffic and many other factors that could make you feel unprepared and make it harder to finish the task. When you spend extra time searching for products or equipment, your routine-and thought-training-will be disrupted.

If you can take the time to think about how you design your office space, amazing things occur. De-cluttering and organizing your office means less time searching as well as more productive time. You won't need to stop your thoughts or conference call train to search for things or get annoyed by the noise that is all around you.

In addition, your colleagues may think you're a naturally neat person. Bonus. Don't be afraid to locate the correct printed version of the RFP as you think about the amount of time you've spent searching through the documents.

Tactic #1: Clean your closet

The toughest part is starting. The process of purging begins by cleaning your office space. Remove everything from your desk and in your file system cabinets and drawers, and decide what's important to keep and what's worth a dab. It's possible to end up with a huge pile of files as well as old conference item but it's worthwhile in the end.

Tactic #2: Clean up the space... as well as ensure it is kept clean

After you've cleaned out your home of clutter You can take note of the dust that built up behind the pile of unutilized office supplies and notes from the past week. Take advantage of this chance to give your desk fresh new look... Extra points, based on whether you're using wood polish or alcohol wipes.

Technique #3: Decide which piles should be left and which pile needs to be disposed of:

Everyone does it: hoarding paper and even designs. "But what if we'll need it in the future? "Trust me, we're not likely to. Certain things are essential and last over time, and may even merit to have their own folder. However, temporary documents are expected to be sorted and date or put in the garbage bin.

It may not sound straightforward, but as you sort it, it becomes simpler. You'll definitely come across things you'd like to keep "just in the event of an emergency" but you should be able that you can let go items that no longer fit your needs. You might find certain gems as well.

Tactic #4: Note them all (seriously and all):

A good label maker will help you save time and effort trying to find things if decide to use it. If it's a printed replica of the map of products or staplers, there's not any time to look for items that have disappeared. Once you're aware of the location of everything, it becomes easy to stay organized.

Tactic #5: Define the areas for the specific items:
Remember this when you mark your items, and you won't have to spend the time searching for new products? If it's time to go back to your desk or drawers to find your valuable items will be able to pinpoint exactly where to put them. Desk supplies, office equipment in this drawer old files in this drawer meeting files on the tray in this one, pen cups on the side, etc.

Tactic #6: Choose the contents of drawers and what staples are left above the your desk
If you're constructing your desk with well-tested objects, determine which should be saved and which will be used frequently. It is suggested to put most of your items away for a minimalist, tidy desk, but for every individual item. It's possible be exhausting seeing the things you're hoping to use, but you never have the chance.

Tactic #7: Make sure that you have whatever is floating in your office:

The vast array of desk organizers that can be found at any store of supplies or supercenter will not go away. No matter if you're traveling using gold, black or stainless steel desk organizers will be useful in the event that you're carrying a reasonable amount of office equipment at your workstation. Some even include an organizer for filing. Nifty.

Tactic #8: Think about your file system in the same way:

Instead of throwing files around without a thought in the cabinets, sort your data in a manner that is most logical to you. This could be through alphabetical organization or by prioritizing the importance of your software. The key is that it makes the sense for you regardless of what method you choose to use.

Tip #9: Prepare documents for meetings:

Make a folder dedicated solely to meetings, no matter if it's collateral, notes, or even comments made on a presentation made by another person. Making a folder specifically for meetings alone means that you'll be able to access everything you need when unclear on the next steps or require guidance to follow up.

10th tactic: Build Project files for people. Project files:

The creation of directories for tasks (team environments) or for individuals (one-on-one work) is dependent on the team dynamics. Similar to the purpose of a conference folder you'll know precisely what file to pull out when an individual in your team needs specific project-related documents.

Tactic #11: Buy an analog inbox for yourself:

Inboxes aren't just for the digital age. Set up your inbox tray at work to be aware that someone is snatching off items even when you're away working at your computer. That also prevents messages/communications away from your carefully planned meetings and project papers from others.

Tactic #12 Note: Separate your hardware from your paper

It may seem not worth the effort but, when you look at your desktop the papers that are a pain to read get relegated to piles. After you've decided on your file system, make an area away from your computer , so that you can remain online and not be reading notes from the meeting the previous week. You don't have to be there at all.

Tactic #13: the odd application of space:

There's an abundance of space for storage between the wall to the window than what is visible to the eye. Do you have an empty windowsill near your desk? Put there your tray for inbox or pencils and save your space. Do you have space to fill the wall with a blank space? There are a myriad of ways to use corkboards for personal items or memos you'd prefer not to take up space on your desk.

The 14th task is to speak out:

Everyone is more productive in an environment that feels as if they are. It doesn't matter if it involves bringing in a tiny quantity of personal items (sparing there) or transforming your office space to reflect your personal style Making yourself feel more comfortable in your home is always a good idea. It doesn't matter if you require your dog's video clips or some distinctive office items... you'll need them.

Tactic #15 Create it into a weekly routine element:

Sure, posting an address label on a document is simple, and then telling people you're going to eliminate the document on Tuesday. Without a schedule the well-intentioned expiration dates will arrive and a reminder for your calendar will be buried with no. Make sure you keep collecting and deleting records once they've been used for their intended goal. Without a set of rules in place, all of these suggestions are not worth the effort.

Tactic #16: Create your own space for storage:

You then organized the files and folders, and out of sight you put away all your other belongings. What are you planning to put in new items? The addition of a desk drawer to your desk is always safe. The majority of desktop organizers have an additional drawer or tray underneath the holders of the file, which means it won't make space.

Tactic #17: Make your own space

Whatever you attempt at work, when you're working doing your work, it's possible to fall into letting things pile throughout the course of the day. However, if setbacks do occur, ensure that you do not compromise on: White Space. Make sure to keep one area of your desk that is open, with the mouse ideally on your side. This way, you'll always have room to work in the event that it seems that everything is going to be shut down.

Tactic #18: Before you go, straighten up:
Take the final five minutes of the day to get rid of all the clutter that has been accumulating throughout the day on your desk. Every evening, you don't need to dust your laptop with a broom or a broom, but a quick clearing out of old coffee cups or your lunch box or any other unorganized files will make it easier to leave your office without stress. It's a fantastic opportunity to unwind from your work and it's always nice to come back in the morning with a tidy desk.

3.2 Organizing your Computer Files
If you use computers all day, you may want to make sure your files are organized in a manner that allows you to locate an item quickly. Make sure you are specific about the names of your files so that if you're

trying to find something urgent you are able to quickly find a particular item. It may not seem like a lot however it could be an excellent time saver.

In our "wired" world keeping your electronic files in order can be an issue.

Beyond the local storage of data on desktops, increasingly more companies are utilizing cloud-based storage for files and business software along with laptops and mobile devices.

The storage problem is made complicated by the necessity for many businesses to share documents among their employees. This usually happens within the office, using an electronic computer (NAS) that is connected to the network or file server.

It is crucial to ensure that they are kept up updated wherever documents are stored. The purpose of managing electronic documents is to ensure you'll find what you're seeking regardless of whether you're searching for years after its initial creation.

A lot of business owners have found themselves in the embarrassing situation of having a client contact them at one point or another, and not being able find the correct invoice or other important documents needed by the customer in a timely manner. The same is the frustration of digging around at the close of the year trying to locate the documents that relate to the accounting firm's account or, even more frustratingly the taxman.

In a shared space the proper management of digital records is especially important when one of your employees is absent (temporarily or for a long time!) you must be able discover any documents that this individual creates or manages effectively.

Data loss concerns that could arise from employees who are angry and leave the company is another reason to safeguard your business's information.

These tips for managing your files will allow you to keep access to your files

Make use of for the Standard System Files Configuration Folders:

Utilize the standard file locations when downloading computer programs. Under Windows the data that is under in the (Drive letter:) Program Files directory reside by default. It's annoying and wasteful to mount the software in another location.

One Place to Store All Documents:

All documents should be placed into a single folder known as heart. The default setting for a user's personal files within the Windows system is to go through the My Documents tab.

Try it with a file-sharing platform. Create one single root folder (for instance "Shared Documents"), and save all documents within the root folder within subfolders. Being the sole place for all documents on the internet helps in locating things easier and also helps to maintain archives and backups.

Create Folders within a Logical Hierarchy

These, as it were are drawers in the filing cabinet in your computer. By using simple language to label your folders at some point, won't want to browse through this list of folders and ask which "TFK" or an obscure abbreviation that you created.

Nest Folders with Folders:

Create additional folders within the primary folders as required. For instance the folder titled "Invoices" might contain folders titled "2018," "2017," and "2016." A folder that is named after clients could comprise the "customer information" as well as "correspondence" documents. The goal is to have every file placed in a folder, instead of a plethora of useless files.

5. Use File Naming Conventions to Follow

A lot of Operating system (such such as Unix) don't need spaces between the name of directories or files therefore, avoid using spaces when mixing machine settings. Instead, use underscores to delimit the file (e.g., Doe John Proposal.doc.) Certain characters, such as > :* are prohibited in Windows name of folders or files. Make use of short names for files to facilitate quick identification and retrieval however, do not overboard with file name limits on length that vary across operating systems. For Windows the maximum path length for an individual file (e.g. drive name + name of the folder + the filename) is the 260-character limit. There are also abbreviations to describe certain words, like"Feb" for Feb.

Be Specific:

Use logical, specific names for electronic files. If you can include dates in file names. The goal is to to identify what the file's purpose is by naming files, without having to open it and examine the file. If, for instance, the text is a letter addressed to the customer telling him that his payment is due and due, you can name it as "overdue 20180110" in place of "mail" since you'll not be able to determine who the letter belongs to without opening the file.

If you plan to share your files via the internet or on portable devices You may need the name of the file to contain more details about the file, as information regarding the file will not be included in the shared file.

For example, if your document resides in My Documents\Invoices\2017\Customers\Doe John 20180416.doc and the file is exchanged or forwarded, then all the recipient will see is the Doe John 20170416.doc and may not be able to say that the file is a customer invoice without opening it.

Preparing for the Journey:

The ideal time to save documents is the moment you begin make it. Thus, practice using the "Save as" option to save your text and then identify it prior to putting it in the correct location.

Get Your Convenience Files Ordered:

If you have a significant number in directories, or even files them up the list of file names by renaming them by using the letter a! or an AA at the beginning of the file's name.

Make sure you clean your files regularly:

Sometimes what's old can be clear like in the example folder above , which is referred to as "Invoices." If not, clean out the old information make sure that the directories remain unaltered.

Make sure you regularly back up your files

When you're copying files to a different drive or disk or disk, establishing and maintaining a routine backup plan is essential.

Effective file management must be an integral part of the overall document management strategy to help your business find the information you need to efficiently manage your electronic documents. A good document management plan should include the entire process of handling documents such as backups, storage, recovery and security.

The search feature is an excellent feature however, the convenience of being able directly to a specific folder or file cannot be compared to. If you're constantly using these methods to manage your files even if you aren't sure the location of something, you have a good idea of where to find it. an immense advantage when you find what you're looking. Effective file management techniques can save time and the company money.

3.3 How to manage your Calendar

If you have an appointment or a briefing to attend during the mid-day or you're working on projects that have deadlines, make them onto your schedule! Even people who do not work in the traditional workplace such as workers or contractors might have several tasks to complete during the same day or prospective clients to talk to. Be sure to not be late or overbooked by tying your email with an online calendar.

It's up to you to determine how you'll use your time. You could be watching Netflix and binge watch all day long however that's not the best thing to do with your time. Also, you must establish boundaries and be out and about inspired. In a sense, you need to determine the right direction to ensure that you achieve the balance between your working and personal time.

It's not regardless of how daunting it may be. It's not as difficult as it sounds and feels. Scheduling and managing your time effectively is the most effective way to create a harmonious balance between your goals in life and work. Here are the top nine efficient methods to lead you to more effective decisions for your balance between work and life along with the organization that follows.

The Plan All Things:

Planning involves organizing everything from your list of things to do of tomorrow to the things you've planned for the coming week. This may sound like a lot however, to be productive and focused it is essential to maintain a the right structure.

It is possible to do this by creating a zero-based calendar. A zero-based calendar is one in which every second of your daily schedule is counted. There's no space left empty on your calendar in this manner. "If you don't schedule something then it's not worthy of to be given your time." For starters every day activities must be scheduled into your calendar. This encompasses both your professional and personal obligations. The first step is to plan the amount of time each item will require to make periods of time. Be sure to make effective use of the gap between. For instance, you could be able to tidy or read your inbox over the 30-minute interval between meetings.

* Break your tasks down into small, easy steps:

It requires more effort to utilize your brain and this is possible to avoid this by simplifying your challenges. Excellence in time management is based on creating a system that is broken down into smaller steps that are easy to understand and don't require massive resource consumption. Entrepreneurs are typically well-known for their capacity to tackle any "complex task" and reduce it into small pieces which makes the remainder of the process simpler to comprehend and implement. For instance, the process of creating an eBook is not a good idea to translate into chunks of calendar size. You must schedule a chunk of time every day to write a specific number of pages , to make an extensive task easier to manage, for instance, allowing two hours to write five pages per day.

* Use the chakra program to color code your calendar:

Coloring your calendar with colors is a proven and effective method for creating harmony and distancing your events within your agenda. Although you are free to color-code your calendar with any color you like, consider color-coding for the chakra before you do. A "chakra" is one of the seven energy points that are located in the body. Each of these points of energy is identified by its color (red or orange green, yellow blue, indigo and violet).

As an example, because red is the chakra of the root that represents health and survival It is logical to utilize that color in every task that is related to the job. You could choose to utilize orange to help with creative work and yellow is a symbol of things that can help you grow and develop; green is for private events like eating lunch with a pal Blue is a color that represents things that stimulate your mind like writing, while indigo is a color for tasks that require your focus. This method of organization will prevent the possibility of becoming overwhelmed. A glance at your calendar will result in a stress-free and healthy day that is easily viewed.

* Consider Plan over Chance:

If you are chasing every possibility, you don't want to over-extend yourself. If you are starting a new business all things from money, attention, and time are scarce. No matter what you do in your life time, money and attention are all in short availability. Make use of your calendar-packed with tasksensure that you concentrate on the plan. The calendar is the instrument to help you achieve success.

Energy and time are most productive when they conform to the values of the organization and the strategy of the company that are determined by the team of the client and the internal requirements.

* Eat that frog

The most effective time management method which is endorsed by Brain Tracy, is where you set your goals for the day prior to anything else, including your top priority (MIT). Research has proven that you are most energetic and focus when you wake up and completing your most difficult job will let you get through your day with the peace and knowledge that it is the most damaging thing to occur to you throughout the day. It's the best moment to avoid distractions as well.

If you have a lot of important tasks, begin by tackling the largest, most difficult and most important one first. Additionally, you must start immediately and keep practicing until you are perfect.

It takes time to understand this. However, you can start your day at nine and work to noon , while preparing your calendar to ensure that you have your main priority throughout the day. Even though you may need to have breaks and usually end your day by noon, this will help establish an order to your day and ensure that your distractions don't interfere with your schedule.

You can try blocking time instead of to-do lists.

While having to-do lists in your schedule can be beneficial but they can also be an area of frustration and stress. For instance, if after your day, you look over your list, and you only cross off some things off what do you think you'll be feeling? Studies have found the fact that nearly 41 percent tasks listed on your list are never accomplished. Additionally, the author of 15 Tips successful people know About Time Management, Kevin Kruse has found that top performers do not count on lists. They create the blocks of their time onto their calendars instead.

For certain tasks Time blocks are just blocks of time. Blocking two hours in the morning to "eat your frog" time," one hour following lunch to tidy up your inbox, or an afternoon time frame for conferences, for instance. In comparison to other schedules that are scheduled, scheduling your time helps you to focus, minimizes distractions, and stops multitasking.

Determine when you are most productive when you begin to be able to schedule that time in your MIT. Record the amount of time it takes you to finish the tasks in order you are able to allocate the appropriate time. The most important thing is to create your plan and adhere to your schedule around these factors. The timing of your work and working out your timetable.

* Create an optional calendar:

The idea here is to create the calendar an "optional" calendar, which includes all of the items that aren't compulsory. A possible elective could be a gathering for friends like a party, for instance or taking classes that will help develop the ability. These are the kinds of events you will manage to attend most likely however, they're not the first thing to leave if you're overwhelmed".

Instead of incorporating and removing things and events from your professional and personal schedules in a continuous manner There's another calendar that is full of possibilities when your main schedule shifts at any minute. You don't need to contemplate how you'll spend this time, because on the "free" calendar, you've already decided on that.

Create unstructured hours into your calendar:

When you're constantly busy and you don't have any free timebecause every minute of the day is a constant cycle of work-- you're maximizing your brain's capabilities and your cognitive capabilities decrease and you are more likely to commit mistakes and have less understanding.

On the other hand, this can add two hours of free time in your day-to-day routine. The time can be used to study, reading meditation, or just taking a look around. This may appear to be unproductive but it could also increase your creative abilities and happiness, and help you become more adaptable. 9. Using proper tools.

In the end, if you truly desire to be in the forefront on your game ensure you have the proper tools to make use of. These tools include A Calendar App. No matter whether the app is Google Calendar, Microsoft Calendar or a Fantastical application, it allows you add events and view your calendar from any place wherever.

Scheduling tool. Calendar is an intelligent calendar that gives intelligent recommendations about the best time, place and how to plan an appointment by using machine learning.

Software that tracks time. If you're looking to manage your calendar, you should understand how to use your time. Tools such as Rescue Time and Smarter Time can track your daily routines.

Apps to keep a note. When you have an idea or thought you can use an app such as Evernote as well as Google Keep to get it out of your mind.

Lists of things-to-do. If you are a fan to-do lists, Things, Remember the Milk and Wunderlist are only a handful of applications that allow you to make, manage and make lists and share them with others.

3.4 How to manage your cell phone

The best way to stay on top of your work is to set up a synchronization of your phone with your email at work and also sync your phone to your calendar. There are plenty of apps to aid you in staying organized on your task at hand.

There's no reason to be alone If your cell phone is a mess. It's not difficult to tell yourself that you'll take it on later- after all the task of organizing your phone could be a very intimidating job. However, getting your phone organized isn't an issue! You'll be amazed at how tidy your cell phone can become after following this two-step procedure.

Clean Your Phone:

Cell phones build up clutter the same way that our home does. A lot of cell phones have software preloaded. Some of them you are unable to uninstall. When we make use of smartphones, the process of downloading files installing a program or taking a photo without thinking is easy. All those little downloads are growing in time. If you have too many duplicate files downloaded will slow your phone, making the task of finding what you want to find more difficult.

We begin the process of cleaning our homes by removing everything are no longer needed. The same principle is applicable to organizing your phone. Here are a few easy ways to clean your phone clean.

Check Your Contacts List:

Do you remember the last time that you browsed through your mobile's address book? In case you've been organizing your contacts list for some time, this is a good way to begin. Go through your contacts and remove the ones that you no longer need. This can take a while, especially in the event that you've never been able to sync your contact list with your address book before.

Your company can move to the next level by updating your contact profile. Make sure you clean the address books by adding any missing email addresses, names as well as last names or other pertinent details. When your most loved contacts call or email you, you can upload a photo to display.

Examine the Applications:

It is possible to download thousands free apps on your mobile phone in just two or three clicks. A lot of us download applications that appear fresh or interesting only to find out they're not useful. While it's best to remove these apps, it's not always the scenario. Most likely, there are more apps in your phone than you'd like or require. Make sure to uninstall apps you no longer need. You might be surprised by the amount you're deleting.

Take a look at your photos:

One of the great aspects of mobile phones is the ability to capture a photo or videos from anywhere and anytime. The process of capturing those memories is a great method to clutter your phone. Do not use your phone to store videos and photographs. In addition to taking up a lot of memory, if your phone is dropped or damage your phone, you could lose your files for ever.

Keep your photos in sync, however by using a digital backup program like Google Photos or iCloud Photos. These applications store your photos in the cloud, automatically that allows you to access them on any computer that has access to an Internet connection. You'll still be able view the images you wish to see at any time but they will not remain in your mobile. This could leave you with an incredible amount of memory, which is close to removing your phones.

Get Your Apps Organized:

The time is now to arrange your apps after uninstalling the ones that you no longer require. The majority of mobile phones offer plenty of options in the area of the best way to organize your applications. But, many people don't utilize this feature to their advantage. It can be extremely frustrating to operate a mobile phone that has a sloppy software. If the applications are hidden away in directories, you may not be able to find them. There are the number of icons that fill the screen and a multitude of icons, the one you require isn't always easy to locate. If you're not sure which one to look for you could spend hours looking on your mobile.

Don't let your phone become the source of your frustration. Or, organize the apps on your smartphone to help make life simpler.

Here are some easy methods to keep your apps to be organized on your phone

Sort Your Apps In Alphabetical Sorting:

If you're seeking a practical method to organize your easy to follow apps, place them alphabetically on your smartphone. Sort them into folders that are alphabetical or lay them out according to the number of apps your phone is loaded with. If you are familiar with the model of device you're searching for, you'll discover it quickly.

Arrange Your Apps based on Function:

The process of separating the apps in folders according to function is another easy method to organize them. It is possible to create as little or as many as you'd like So think about the best solution for you. You can also look around on the internet and see what other people have done!

There are a variety of categories that could be included, including applications for bank banking, such as bills-for-banks as well as payment options that can be made digitally and bill pay applications.

Social media like Snapchat, Twitter, Instagram and LinkedIn.

Software for photo and video which can edit and capture digital media.

Music and Media for Spotify, YouTube, Apple Music and other streaming applications.

Apps-for all the games you love on your phone.

Health and fitness trackers for calories, workout apps and more.

Family Command Center for all your schedules, to-do lists Notes, and other applications that will help you stay in touch with your family and manage your home.

Sort Your Apps By How You Use Them:

If you wish to use your handset in an more practical way, you must sort your apps according to the amount of use they receive. Create a folder of your most used applications in the middle and front of your phone. Drag the icons into. No matter if you're using your smartphone to check the news, stay in contact with your loved ones or to learn new skills, this method can be beneficial to you.

It shouldn't be a daunting task to organize your mobile phone. By systematically removing apps pictures, apps, and unnecessary documents, you'll be able to identify what's essential and arrange it in a manner that's logical for you. Then, you'll be able to relax on your phone with no pressure of finding items you require.

3.5 Maintaining your vehicle:

It is crucial to ensure that your vehicle is clean and neat for those with an occupation that requires them to work in their car like plumbers or landscapers. You'll need to be able to locate things quickly when working, so make sure to arrange any tools or objects you'll need within your vehicle to avoid chaos, which could cause items to be lost or not found.

Chapter 7: Importance organizing your life

Organising your home, office and even your the mind can boost your relationship, happiness as well as the other five things in your daily life. A mountain of laundry and endless tasks can be exhausting and can disrupt every aspect that you live, and not only your routine or tidy home. "Getting organised at the conclusion of the day is all about making time for yourself as well as helping you live an enlightened life. getting rid of clutter can aid you in making healthier decisions, improve your relationships and can even boost your fitness.

4.1 Reduce Depression and Stress

Homeowners who saw their home in a negative light as "cluttered" or filled with "unfinished work" were more exhausted, stressed, as well as had higher concentrations cortisol than those who believed their home was "restful" or "restorative," If you arrive home to a mountain of items or a to-do list, it might hinder the natural decrease in cortisol all day long, experts claim. The result can impact your mood, health, sleep, and much more. Making the effort to clear the laundry piles, look through your papers and tidy your living space is not just about clearing out the physical clutter, but can also make you feel more relaxed and relaxed.

Strategies to manage your time in the event of depression:

Even on the worst mental health day, here are five strategies to get through the mess.

1. The perfectionism that is thrown out the window:

Even at their lowest there is a tendency to be pushed to look "perfect." In the past, it has come to be aware that mental health and perfection situations are usually directly in opposition. It is better to be aware that during the winter months, a house may not appear perfect. You'll have to put up with the sloppy dust bunny who might wander into your home even if everything is in order.

It's not always about perfect to be organized "It's about the normal living quality. Everyone has different standards. As long as the arranged environment meets the standards and doesn't interfere with a range of living that is causing or threatening to the existence of the individual, the person is likely to get approval and peace from it. "Let let go of the idea of" good, "and instead reach for an organization level that doesn't compromise any quality of living.

2. Break it up into bite-sized pieces

Since stress can be a huge problem for people with mental health issues such as anxiety, it is recommended to break up an organizational project into digestible chunks.

Divide the entire project into small pieces and determine the importance of each section starting at the level that will ease the most stress.

"The objective is to help the person to understand the whole process and assist them in understanding the best way to tackle it in a way that is manageable." Also, dedicate fifteen to twenty minutes each day to things which need to be accomplished for example, like doing the laundry or sorting the mail.

A little effort is often enough to boost the mind and help build momentum that can boost a positive feeling. However, if you're dealing with mental health issues it isn't always the scenario. Consider yourself grateful if you are absent from work or only have 10 minutes to devote.

3. Eliminating things that don't benefit you:

Physical clutter can create mental clutter especially if your life and your space has been consumed by that clutter.

"It's not about getting organized but about how you can let go and let go of guilt or shame about your possessions. After this it's not often an issue.

It is recommended that you consider the importance of thinking about how an item is "valuable," as opposed to an item you believe could be worth a lot of money due to the fear of or other emotions.

4. Remove distractions:

Being extremely sensitive means that you're suffering from an issue with your sensory system that is very easy to become overwhelmed. A high volume, a lot of clutter and a plain-sight to-do lists can quickly sever your focus and drag away from the task your working on.

It is recommended that you also create a space that is as peaceful as you can through tranquility and peace when you organize. If you're certain you won't be distracted You should reserve an amount of time.

5. Imagine the final product:

Seasonal depression is the most prevalent out of all mental health disorders that drain off any need to tidy or organize their lives since depression can cause the impression of being defeated. The importance of focusing on the end purpose is vital.

"People who are suffering from disorder are overloaded by mind and body and the need to go to a support group and mindfulness services is essential to recover. Help is crucial.

A WAY TO BE HAPPY IF You're Depressed:

Being content can be the most crucial thing you can do to improve your overall health, which makes it as crucial to your eating habits and exercise. If you don't feel like yourself lately, don't worry. Recognizing that life isn't easy and that sometimes the unexpected can happen, here are some strategies to get you back to smiling.

Play a game (Not on Your Mobile and Laptop):

Gather your family Invite your friends and enjoy a night at the field. You'll not only be in great group of people, but also friendly rivalry ensures fun and laughter.

Smile

Smile whenever you are in doubt! Smiles are not just healthy but it also helps ease anxiety, improve your mood and releases endorphins.

Get Walking:

If at home or at work you feel that something isn't going right, go out and walk. It doesn't need to be long, but you'll enjoy breath of fresh air as well as clear your head by taking a short walk.

Make a call to a friend:

Don't send texts; Contact! A call to a trusted acquaintance is an excellent way to chat with someone whom you trust with your issues and receive guidance.

Try something different by switching things around:

Get off the beaten track:

Explore a new fitness class and/or restaurant or take on a new working route.

Unplug:

Take a break from your hectic schedule by switching off your gadgets and turning off Facebook and Twitter for at least a moment or two minutes.

Sing (Out Loud):

You can sing any time you want in the shower in your car. You can be certain that you'll feel more relaxed -when you sign an album deal or not. it.

Volunteer:

It's hard to beat the feeling of knowing that you are doing something to help others. Help make the difference by visiting Volunteer Match, and meet some new friends during the process.

Write a list of gratitude:

Concentrating on the negative aspects or the things you're not able to have is often simple. Get your mood up and running by writing down things you're thankful for regardless of size.

Eat Up:

Begin cooking your Fava beans now, and they will can make you feel happy! Since this legume is loaded with significant amounts of the amino acid, known by the name L-dopa (dopamine) It improves your mood and decrease depression.

Practice Yoga

Yoga assists in relaxing your mind.

Have a break:

Perhaps you're in need of an escape. Make time to explore around your neighborhood instead of planning a trip. A trip to a new place might be just what you're looking for to recharge and appreciate the world all around you.

Declutter

Get organized. To have a fresh start. The removal of mess and having your space changed up will make it feel fresh. This is also a ideal base from which to take off.

4.2 help you eat Healthier

For those who have spent just only 10 minutes working in a clean environment are two times more likely to select an apple instead of a chocolate bar than people who spend the identical amount of time in a filthy workspace, which suggests that organization can help people be healthier eaters. The stress of clutter is felt by the brain, which means you're more likely to turn to ways to cope such as more comfort food or eating too much when you're in a clean and tidy environment.

Tips to assist both you and your loved ones members eat healthier:

Learn these basic suggestions to help your family take a step-by step approach to healthy eating. When you organize your eating habits in this manner your life will become simpler.

Let children have fun trying out different fruits and veggies. Every week, they can choose a food item or vegetables from the store and decide how to cook it , or create a healthy dish.

Whole grains are a great option! Choose whole grain foods such as whole-wheat bread brown rice, rye bread popcorn, oatmeal, and whole grain cereals.

If you're like me, some fats are more beneficial than others. In lieu of butter or other strong fats, use liquid vegetable oils like corn, canola and sesame oils, safflower, and sunflower oils when you can.

Let your children develop healthy habits in their early years that can provide lifetime benefits. Set the example for them and make it fun and involve the whole family in the changes to their lifestyle.

Fish, chicken and beans are good protein sources. Remove the skin from poultry and take off all visible fat. Reduce it to once time if you are eating red meat. Keep portions small and pick the most slim cuts.

Look up nutritional labels on food items. Choose healthy food items that contain nutrients like minerals, vitamins, as well as the dietary fiber, but avoid sodium, sugars added as well as saturated fats and trans-fats.

You are in control of portions and ingredients when you cook at home, which is why you should try for cooking more frequently at home instead of having eating out.

Make sure you have fresh fruit and cut-up or no-chop veggies in your pantry for snacks. If they're readily available your family is more likely pick up vegetables and fruits instead of other foods.

Consume fish that has fat acids that are rich in omega-3. Fish with oily oils like albacore, mackerel and salmon tuna and trout are excellent choices.

Get your family talking about Sneaky Salt! Make the commitment and discover ways to reduce the sodium consumption of your family. A lot of sodium in our diet comes from processed and restaurant food items, not your salt shaker!

A tiny pound of seeds or nuts can be a nutritious, delicious snack. Find nuts that are not salted or slightly salted. The best choices are hazelnuts, almonds, pecans, peanuts, pistachios and walnuts.

In general, they are low in sodium and calories fruit and vegetables are packed with minerals and fibre. Fresh frozen, canned, or frozen foods are all healthy alternatives, so be sure to check the labels to make informed decisions.

Utilizing dried or fresh spices and herbs instead of salt during cooking, or making a salt-free blend of seasoning. To flavor the food you cook you can add a squeeze of fresh lime or lemon.

Pack your healthy snacks yourself. Cut up fruits and vegetables in portions-sized containers for quick and healthy snacks in the car without adding sodium and sugar.

Do you know about the "Salty Six? These six foods are known to contribute the most salt to our diets for our kids. Compare the labels on food items in making healthy choices for your kids.

Cook your vegetables in nutritious ways that enhance their natural flavors, like grilling, roasting and steaming, baking and baking. You'll require less (if you have any) salt, and you can transform even the most uninterested vegetable child

Let our hearts be your guide when shopping for grocery items. Choose foods that have the Heart-Check seal of the United States' specific Association to make better choice in your food.

Instead of sodas that are sweetened with sugar or tea opt for sparkling water, tea that isn't sweetened or sugar-free drinks. To enhance the flavor, include lime, lemon, or berries to drinks.

Limit traditional sweets to celebrations and try fruit to eat for dessert every day. Make a tasty smoothie, perfectly blended berry, yogurt, or even a cooked apple with a spiced crust or pear!

Instead of deep-frying food, which can result in a significant amount of calories and unhealthy fats, use healthier cooking methods that use little or no solid fats, like grilling, roasting, baking or steaming.

Plant vegetables and fruits in your backyard. The children are more inclined experiment with something that they have learned about.

Make time for planning healthy meals every week. To make budgeting and preparation easier, make sure you keep your menus, grocery lists and coupons in one spot.

Serving size doesn't have to be the same as the dimensions of the section. Check the serving size and servings per container. Two or more servings may be equivalent to what appear to be a normal serving.

Let your children play in the kitchen! If they're active they'll be engaged in eating healthy meals. Set them up with tasks that are appropriate for their age and make sure they have a step stool in their bag.

To make a quick and simple food, choose dried or frozen varieties of fish or poultry. Limit the sodium content and opt for the options that are that are bottled in water.

Every week, make a meatless dish. Consider a lasagna with veggies or even a mushroom-based burger served on portabella! Beans and vegetables can enhance meals with fiber, protein, and other nutrients.

Lobby to ensure that children are healthier. Make sure that children are offered healthy food choices in the schools and childcare centers. Make contact with public officials, and let your voice be heard.

It might seem difficult to be healthy and balanced with a tight budget, however it is possible! The majority of vegetables (beans or peas) cost less than $1 for a serving.

Beware of sugars that are added. They add calories, but do not offer any nutritional value. Most of us are aware that soft drinks and drinks sweetened with sugar are the most common source of sugar added.

Enjoy the rainbow. Food that is as diverse as you can in a day is an enjoyable and tasty way to make sure that everyone has a diverse selection of fresh fruits and vegetables.

4.3 It helps improve your Relations

Family relationships that are happy with your family and friends is essential in preventing illness and depression But a messy life can put a strain on these bonds. Unorganized clutter can cause tension and conflict between couples. The time spent trying to find missing items could be a distraction from spending time with your loved ones. A messy home may discourage you from inviting friends to visit. Unorganized living can cause shame and embarrassment, forming an emotional and physical boundary surrounding you, which prevents your guests from being allowed to access your home. A girls' meeting can provide the incentive you need to keep your home neat and tidy.

Tidy home, happy spouse? This may sound like a silly little adage however, it could provide a surprising amount of truth.

In a survey from 2016 by newly separated couples the most common reason for divorces, which was third place after being in a relationship and breaking up, according to 30 percent of respondents, was referred to as "housework disagreements." A similar survey conducted from Pew Research Center found that more than half of married couples said that having a shared the chores of the household was "very essential" for a happy marriage.

Couples today are often exhausted trying to manage everything including demanding jobs, children (if they have children) and relationships with their family and friends and relationships with one another and their families, grocery shopping, meal prep and cleaning, keeping in the middle of bills all while attempting to take care of their physical and mental well-being. They give priority to and only talk about what is required in any given day. The rest of the work should be left to the last minute -and that includes tidying up.

Maintaining a clean and tidy home can be quite overwhelming and is easy to slip through the cracks of those with lots of things to attend to. Since keeping the home clean isn't a priority, it's put aside in favor of more urgent issues, like working on time."

In certain couples, both spouses have a common desire to be organized but they cannot figure out enough time or energy to accomplish it. Certain couples face a unique situation: one spouse is a neat freak who is frustrated by the mess of their living spaces and the other is not bothered by the mess- or loves it. The difference in style and needs certainly causes tensions between spouses.

Cleaning your house may seem like a minor concern in comparison to completing a major deadline project or taking sick children for a visit to the physician. However, a messy living space's impact on your life can seriously harm the physical and mental health of your family and make you feel anxious, over-stressed, anxious and even guilty.

Stress and anxiety can impact your partner's manner in which they treat you. which can make you less patient and accommodating , and more likely to be prone to snippiness negative nitpicking and passive aggressive behaviors.

The sight of a lot of clutter can cause you to feel overwhelmed. It's difficult to know where to begin, so you simply don't even begin. The house feels like its task is never done and never will be finished.

A messy house can be overwhelming, making us feel unable and anxious. Many people have different notions about where an object is located in the house. It can be frustrating when it's impossible to locate an item and tensions begin to build within the relationships. It results in cluttered counters or drawers that are overflowing with clutter, as well as the same'lost' objects that are purchased repeatedly.

It's not about committing an entire weekend to getting rid of every month's garbage and then letting it slowly grow. The goal is to find a place for every item and developing a system you can manage. The initial hurdle, particularly in the case of a large amount of things, can be challenging but the reward is often significant.

Once a home is well-organized and simple to maintain A lot of stress is removed from daily life and from your relationship, via connection. A clean space opens the way for couples to spend more time with each other, both mentally and physically. The decluttering process in the home allows couples to be more vigilant in all other areas of their lives, just so that they can have the time and space to spend time with each other and the life you've made together.

If both parties agree to this idea within relationships, it allows them to spend more

time and money on shared experiences ,
and also the time to talk about their
dreams, fantasize, and talk to one another.
If, for instance, you have four shirts to wash,
rather than two hundred it means you'll
have more time with your companion. This
is due to the changing of routines
themselves into an opportunity to connect
with your friends in the same series. It is
possible to catch up on the day's events
while washing the dishes or getting your
children involved in the process of folding
laundry.

The time of year where many people make
an effort to organize and get rid of clutter,
but the only way to keep the process going
instead of slipping back into the old ways of
living is to make sure that every time you
introduce something new to your home, be
conscious. Be aware of whether you're
moving or adding something to, and choose
the best storage space. You should each be
accountable to only store things that will
help you achieve your vision.

4.3.1 Tips to Restore your relationships from
clutter:

There are some tips to help you restore your relationship, if it's getting ruined by clutter and disorder.

1. Be aware of your Heart

If you find yourself in a situation of tension within your family due to decluttering and organizing, begin listening from your heart. Instead of worrying about what to do or what you want to accomplish take the time to listen intently to other people's thoughts without accusing, judging, or judging. What do they'd like to see or feel? Where would they like to reside and to be entitled to their belongings?

If you think you have identified a desire then confirm it to the person who spoke by re-reading it. For example If a member of your family tells you, "I hate it when I take all my things out to finish a task and then you have to put it away in a place where I'm unable to find it" you could inquire, "Do you mean you wish to keep everything in the open till the task is completed or would you prefer to have the chance to store all the materials in storage?"

2. Accommodate Various Clutter Styles:

The reality is that not everyone at home is awash with the same level of clutter. It is possible that you want every surface that are on your walls clear of clutter and furnishings or decor to be arranged However, your spouse may like to have an abundance of books, knick-knacks and other items around the room, as well as rooms filled with furniture and artwork. Think about naming a room or even an space in the room where every family member has for themselves, and that is able to decorate in the how they'd like. If you think the space to be messy it is essential to feel like you have control and belonging to the house with everyone you share it with.

3. The Homeless Things Box:

In our hectic lives, it's common for items to move between rooms or within and out of homes and without having a "home" assigned. Think about creating a bag basket or box of "Homeless things" for all the items that are scattered throughout your home. Maybe you can establish a routine that every family member look over the container at the end of dinner, or every week, and take away the belongings that belong to them.

You will notice as time passes, which things are stored in the container, such as pens, chargers, documents, etc. These are important data can be used to create storage systems that can store these items and provide them with a permanent home!

In addition, you can periodically inform people that anything not removed from the container will be taken to the thrift shop, be reused, or put in the garbage on a particular date and time.

4. Decluttering to improve health for the family:

It's an effective means to help you create the living and home you'd like for each family member. For you all it's a means to acknowledge and process your feelings about different objects and the meaning they have. It's a way for you to provide your physical and mental room to the family members so that their talents and passions can develop.

4.4 Enhance Your Productivity

Distractions can be distracting, and research suggests that it may hinder your concentration when you are looking at multiple objects at the same time can overload your visual cortex and impedes the processing capacity of your brain. Cleaning your desk will be sure be rewarded in the workplace however the benefits are not finished there. Sometimes, inability to make time is the biggest obstacle to a healthy lifestyle. You're more efficient and productive when you are well-prepared at work. That means you'll be able to finish work in an appropriate time and then go home. This allows you to have enough time to workout, cook nutritious meals, relax and rest more.

Decluttering techniques to boost your productivity:

The main enemy of effectiveness is Clutter. But it's not always the most effective method to unwind or spark a fresh idea to organize your work space. There are some techniques that can assist us to work more efficiently. They are "tricks" because they aid us in getting into proper mindset. The first benefit is that they help tidy things up, but the main benefit is being better at letting suggestions in, committed to accomplishing tasks and more calm.

1. Incorporate the habit of removing garbage:

A lot of junk in at work is among the biggest inhibitors to productivity. There's a unique mental shift that takes place when you remove it. The brain does not have to handle the sheer magnitude of the removal. The act of getting rid of things will set the mood for the day. It is also possible to compose more precisely or finally eliminate your inbox. (Just take your garbage away and stop filling the landfill.)

2. Buy any of the following organizers:

Put things in their correct place in the event that you are feeling disorganized. In order to do this you'll need a method to arrange your stuff (if you were not throwing things around). Take an in-depth look at your office. If you notice anything that is "sitting out" you might want to consider adding shelves like this cart or storage unit. They're doing amazing things. You must ensure that you have a space to relax inside your workplace.

3. Swap your desk:

The act of switching the desk can have an effect of cleaning even if it takes longer than simply clearing the clutter. It also allows you to rearrange your workspace and consider what you require. The third benefit is that you'll be inspired to be more productive by the new furniture. (The old desk was probably somewhat stained by coffee.) There are some who might appreciate this new Teknion Upstage model due to its cool design which is far more significant than what you believe.

4. Open some space:
Make sure you have some open room in your workplace and then leave it as is. In an advertisement or brochure, it's as empty space. The mind will feel more at ease when you fill the space with fresh ideas. In a case of extremes One person had to remove everything, including a desk and chair, keyboard, laptop keyboard and (of of course) the speakers in his office. And he claimed that he was better because of it.

5. Declutter your virtual desktop:

If you're anything like the majority people, then your laptop, computer laptop, tablet, or computer are likely to accumulate more games. Take the time to eliminate those that you do not need and then get them reduced. It can be used for your display of the main screen as well as your app's settings. Digital decluttering assists you think more clearer. Check your contacts list in addition to the above and clean it up to see if it can help. You should be at a point where you are feeling clear on the internet.

6. Get rid of the dirt:
You've cleared out your trash and organized the things you need to and cleared your office. Another thing you can do is perform some additional cleaning. A thorough clean of any spills on your desk and carpet and dusting can affect your mood. It's all too obvious, isn't it? Take note of the fact that you're doing this in order to motivate you to do more efficiently. Imagine how you can are able to start fresh on this. Connect the dirt removal to the need to increase efficiency.

4.5 Aids in sleeping better

Cleanliness equals lesser stress which naturally, results in more restful sleep. However, keeping your bedroom tidy could help your sleep in different ways. Those who clean their beds each day are more likely feel comfortable and have a good sleep regularly 75% of those reported having a great night's rest in a bed that was clean and fresh, as they were more relaxed physically, as per an analysis conducted of the National Sleep Foundation. These experts suggest that you remain organized prior to bed and also spruce up you pillows, and cleaning your bedding. The chaos of your day can make you carry the any last-minute tasks, like making payments or writing emails and emails, to your bedroom. This could cause you to stay up later and cause you to snore more. A more organised life will provide your bedroom with a place for rest (and sexual activity!).

When you've gone bed feeling somewhat unhappy over the state of your bedroom there's a good chance that your night was filled with clutter. "Before sleeping the last things we look at (or contemplate) as well as the very first thing we look at upon waking influence our lives for the rest of our life."

The physical clutter that interferes with sleeping:

In the event that your room is filled with clutter, it'll subconsciously or not "weigh" on your. There's a well-known phrase that says "Home Harmony is Harmony." This can prevent your battery from fully charging over the course of a night. If you awake, and the surroundings begin to decrease, it could influence your wellbeing as you go through the rest of your day. The bed and the dormitory should be a sanctuary to recharge your body, mind, and your soul. The hodgepodge is something that has to be accomplished while the brain is in a state of clutter. The mind may be able to ignore the clutter at a conscious level since it's been there for so long, however, the mind desires to complete the task at unconsciously. It doesn't matter if we know of it, these conditions can make us feel overwhelmed and down or anxious.

In addition, the absence of of clutter give you the subconscious capacity to relax and ease anxiety Additionally, it allows you to be more connected to your spouse. The goal of the bedroom is to be able to communicate with your partner and relax. Additionally adding something else to the room can instantly diminish the strength and strength of these two essential things in our lives.

Things that could disrupt rest:
Technology Devices If you are able to remove any thing from your bedroom by using an LCD TV, you'll feel more at ease. Every day our lives, we're so connected to technology that our minds are extremely active. According to research from recent times tablets, smartphones, and computers emit blue light that stimulates the brain and can make it difficult to sleep after gazing at these screens.

Business Documents: Establishing an office-life line. You could be distracted from sleeping by reviewing bills, to-do lists, and other papers need to be dealt with.
Bookshelves full of books: Every book contains ideas and content that you've read , or an urge to read things you've not read yet but you feel you ought to have. All of

these can keep your mind busy until you go to sleep.

The stimulating colors and artwork: Anything you take a look at that is thrilling incredible, amazing, and captivating will stimulate your mind instead of helping you relax. Pick art that is tranquil soothing colors, soft shades, and serene scenes.
Family and Friends Photos If you see the photos which make you feel relaxed and serene, save them. However, if you're having problems with these people or are annoyed Remove their pictures from your space.

messy spaces: Although we're not able to keep our homes clean and neat every day If you've got dirty clothes lying around and laundry that needs to be put away or piles of clutter on the floor instead of the gorgeous bed linens, with a blush, you'll focus on the mess, which isn't the ideal way to begin your day. Clean the walls and floors as clean as you can so you can keep your space an oasis of peace and peace, not one where tension and chaos.

Big Furniture "Large furnishings are among the most significant issues we face "If you own a huge armoire in front of your door, you could be imagining that it's about collapse upon you. Clean the space to allow space for tranquil energy. "Space Under the Bed: It is advised to leave the area under the bed empty in order to create space for flow of energy. "If things are stacked in a closet, packed into drawers, or set over the mattress... it's impossible to quickly find the things you require that could make you angry. Make sure to clear your space to keep things you truly enjoy.

Light Clutter: In the last 30-60 minutes prior to going to sleeping, you will experience a gentle light. Lights that flicker are soothing to the brain and can help you allow you to relax. Find the most dark curtains that you can get to ensure you get a better night's sleep and keep you awake during the daytime hours of the sunlight.

Noise Clutter: A great sleeping space is dark and peaceful. If outside noises are echoing within your room, then you might have to open the windows or hang up a large drape.

When your appliances are constantly humming and heaters are on and off throughout the night, you should consider purchasing an audio machine that is white or fan.